Cornerstones
for Writing

Teacher's Book
Year 4

Alison Green, Jill Hurlstone
and Jane Woods

Series Editor
Jean Glasberg

CAMBRIDGE
UNIVERSITY PRESS

Contents

Introduction

'Write about something you did in the holidays.' As most teachers know, this kind of instruction usually leads to uninspiring results: unstructured writing with no clear beginning or ending, which is often repetitive or a mix of fact and fantasy. Even worse, it can lead to blank sheets of paper and demoralised children. *Cornerstones for Writing* provides both teacher and children with the guidance they need to proceed step by step, with confidence, to a written text. It fully supports the writing objectives in the National Literacy Strategy.

In many classrooms, excellent work is being done to help children write fluently and effectively. However, for all too many children, success in writing continues to trail significantly behind that in reading. This resource aims to narrow the gap between reading and writing ability in a number of ways:

- by providing carefully selected texts as models, so that children learn the benefits of reading as authors and writing as readers;
- by helping children to identify key structural and linguistic features of important text types;
- by taking children step by step through the processes used by successful writers;
- by motivating children through establishing a clear audience and purpose for writing.

Cornerstones for Writing components

The resource has the following components:

Writing Models OHT Pack *or* Poster Pack

The OHT pack contains 32 overhead transparencies, which can be used with any overhead projector to display texts to the whole class. As an alternative, the same material is available in a poster pack of 16 double-sided A1 posters, in a 'write-on-wipe-off' format. Both the OHT pack and poster pack comprise:

- example texts from a variety of sources, which provide models for each of the different types of writing covered within the resource;
- versions of planning frameworks which appear in the copymasters, allowing the teacher to model planning with the whole class;
- where appropriate, activities for the whole class which draw attention to particular features of writing.

Notes on how to use each OHT or poster can be found in the instructions for each session within this teacher's book.

Teacher's Book

The teacher's book contains:

- notes to help you conduct the shared sessions for each step of the writing process; these are arranged in six units of work, covering the year;
- summaries of the group or independent follow-up activities, most of which are set out in the pupil's book (see below);
- suggestions for a guided focus for each group session ('guided group support');
- photocopy masters for group work;
- homework suggestions to support each unit;
- self-assessment sheets to allow children to evaluate their success with each unit;
- facsimiles of the text extracts in the OHT pack/poster pack, to help your planning.

Pupil's Book

The pupil's book provides activities to follow up and reinforce the teaching in the shared sessions. Most of these activities relate to the early stages of the writing process (i.e. **Modelling** – see below), as once the writing is well under way the children will be focusing on their own compositions.

Five steps to writing

For children to write confidently, they need to be taught a generic procedure which they can apply to <u>any</u> writing task. The *Cornerstones for Writing* five-step process helps young authors to approach their writing just as a skilled adult would. These five steps are outlined below:

1 Modelling

This step provides children with a successful 'how to' model for constructing their own text. Using the appropriate model text(s) from the OHT or poster pack, you should demonstrate how to map out a structural framework and identify linguistic features. Subsequent group activities encourage the children to remember and use this model for their own future writing.

2 Planning

Planning is an excellent method of establishing and keeping control. If children know how to plan in detail, and have practised the skill frequently enough for it to become familiar, they are likely to write more effectively.

Planning frameworks are helpful for children of most ages and abilities, especially when using one that has been problem-solved in class from a model text. Over a number of units, the children will learn the generic skill of 'finding' a suitable framework for writing and then using it to organise content. This is much more useful than becoming over-reliant on published 'writing frames', which, when used without real understanding on the part of the children, may leave some to flounder when the frame is taken away.

3 Drafting

Drafting is the process of getting words and ideas down on paper in provisional form, without worrying too much about elegance of expression or organisation of the pages. With the planning already done, the children are free to concentrate on the writing itself.

4 Revising and editing

Revising focuses on the content and style of a text, and allows the children to check that they have written everything that needed to be written, and are satisfied with it. It also provides an opportunity to evaluate the text from the viewpoint of the intended reader, and make any changes necessary to address the reader's needs. Editing focuses on accurate spelling and punctuation, to ensure effective communication of the author's ideas to the reader.

This step usually requires the most diplomatic handling by the teacher. The children have worked hard to produce their texts, and sometimes fail to see the point of doing any more work. It is very important, therefore, to show how improvements can be made. This will be facilitated by frequent reading and re-reading aloud to bring out 'before and after' contrasts. A really successful shared experience of revising and editing will often convert young writers away from a haphazard 'one-go' approach.

5 Publishing

Publishing is the final step in the process, where the text is produced in the form in which it will reach its intended audience. This may be done by, for example, the posting of a letter, the performance of a poem or the creation of an attractive classroom display. At this stage the arrangement of words on pages and the inclusion of illustrations, diagrams and other displayed material become most important.

Ensuring that the finished text reaches its intended audience in polished form validates the whole process. Even under great pressure of time, teachers ignore this at their peril! If the children's work never reaches an audience beyond their teacher, it is hardly surprising that they do not become audience-aware, and do not learn to craft texts for a variety of audiences and purposes. Young writers are often inspired by the pride and success they feel when they see their work word-processed, or neatly copied and displayed.

Teaching the five steps

Modelling

Conducting a shared modelling session

The nature of a shared modelling session is specific to each different text type, so much more detailed guidance is given in the shared session notes for each unit.

Modelling in group work

The children use a range of activities in the pupil's book and, where appropriate, on copymasters to familiarise themselves with the structure and features of the text type.

Planning

Conducting a shared planning session

Before the writing begins, it is essential that children know for whom they are writing, why they are writing, and how the outcome of their work will be 'published'. Where possible, share these decisions with the children to enhance motivation. Give them a deadline for producing the texts, tell them how much time and support will be available and whether they should write individually, in pairs or in groups.

Purpose and audience are crucial to the content, tone and length of the final document. Spend some time discussing and considering the needs of the audience: make preliminary decisions about how complicated the vocabulary can be, how formal the tone should be, etc.

Establish the intended method of publication. (This is for the children's independent writing – although the class text could also be published if you wish.) For example, the finished writing could be:

- made into a booklet for younger children;
- published in the school magazine;
- made into a classroom display;
- typed up as a letter to a specific recipient;
- read out in assembly.

Make brief notes of your decisions on these issues and keep them on display to refer back to during the writing process. Plan the shared text together with the children and, similarly, display the class plan as a model for their own plans.

Planning in group work

The children follow the same procedure as in the shared session, and plan their own texts. They work from either planning frameworks on copymasters or prompts in the pupil's book. It may be helpful to conduct a guided group session for this step with the less able children. This will ensure that they have a firm basis to work from once drafting begins (see **Guided focus suggestions** on page 9).

Drafting

Conducting a shared drafting session

It is strongly recommended that drafts be written on large sheets of paper so they can be kept for subsequent revising, and examined again alongside the finished text. It is often helpful for children to see the entire 'evolution' of a piece of writing.

Especially in their early experiences, it is difficult for young writers to be disciplined enough to stick to a plan. Read back each section of planning notes to the children as you go along and involve them in composing sentences to build and elaborate the text. Keep them firmly on track by referring repeatedly to what they have already decided to do, rejecting suggestions that would move away from this. (Occasionally, however, you may wish to add in an inspired 'extra' to make the point that, although planning is a very useful procedure, texts are not set in stone until published.)

Drafting may sometimes be slow to gain momentum – you may need to suggest some alternatives for discussion. Children often love to vote on the best choice from a number of strong suggestions. Good ideas which are not used in the shared text can be used in the children's own writing.

When drafting, do not worry about some sentences being too informal, or about words that do not quite fit – you need some material for improving in the revising and editing step. Often, if there are too many conflicting ideas, or if the children are becoming bogged down in how to write a particular part of the text, it is best to scribble something provisional and move on quickly. Problems can be underlined and returned to later. Often the solution to a writing problem becomes clearer as the text progresses.

Keep reading the text back to the children so that they establish a 'feel' for its tone and flow. Young writers often need to hear their writing read aloud in order to appreciate fully its length, sentence structure, etc.

'Time out' discussions may help to promote the full involvement of all the children during shared sessions. The use of small wipe-off boards for children to write and show their contributions may overcome any reluctance to speak aloud. It may also help to maintain pace in a lesson – especially if the children can be kept thinking and writing while you scribe an agreed sentence.

Finally, remember that the teacher is in charge of the shared text! Do not be afraid to 'drive' or control the piece to make a point or fulfil an objective. Explain and discuss how you are thinking as you work. As children gain in experience and confidence you will undoubtedly wish to involve them more collaboratively at times, but shared writing remains the main vehicle for teacher demonstration of writing skills.

Drafting in group work

It is often a good idea for the children to work in pairs and to tell their partner what they intend to write before writing it down. Verbalising their thoughts first can help the writing process and deters the children from making assumptions about the knowledge of the reader. Their partner will inevitably ask 'Why?', 'How?' and 'When?' if things are not clear to them.

It may be helpful to conduct a guided group session for this step with the less able or average children. These children will need some support with 'getting the language flowing' for a specific text type or audience (see **Guided focus suggestions** on page 9).

Revising and editing

Conducting a shared revising and editing session

Display the first draft. Discuss its effectiveness in relation to the main features of the text type, the original purpose for writing, the intended audience and so on. Praise its strengths, but be realistic about any problems or weaknesses. Remind the children that even professional authors have to revise and edit their work in order to make it worth publishing.

Straight away, deal with any parts of the text that were marked 'to come back to' while the first draft was being written. Use a new colour of pen so that changes are obvious. Next, ask the children to check the class plan and any additional materials (such as posters made in previous sessions) to ensure that the content includes everything that was planned. Discuss whether any additional content is needed at this stage. Then examine the style, flow and tone of the text. Decide whether the right words have been used, and whether any sentences need to be altered.

Sometimes a class will stoutly deny that there are any improvements to be made. Be prepared with two or three points that you are going to insist that they address. Also, be prepared to suggest some alternative improvements for them to evaluate and select from. Gradually, as they gain faith in this part of the process, the children will become more enthusiastic and discerning in their contributions.

You should also consider how well the text addresses the needs of its intended audience. Encourage the class to pretend that they are reading the work for the first time, 'in role' as members of this audience. Help the children to appreciate that a piece of writing is effective only if the intended audience can read or understand it.

Make a final check of spelling and grammar. Decide beforehand, according to your teaching objectives, how much responsibility you expect the children to take for ensuring the final standard of correctness in the shared text. Often it will be you, as scribe, who automatically assumes most editorial responsibility. Having made any necessary teaching points, remaining corrections should not take up too much time.

It can sometimes be very useful to use one of the children's drafts for a shared revision session. Children are often pleased that their work is being held up as an example (it is, of course, important to praise the work before revising and editing begins). Type out the child's work in advance, correcting any spelling, punctuation or other errors that are not to be part of the revising focus.

Revising and editing in group work

In groups, children 'echo' the revising and editing process, as for the other steps. It may be helpful to give them a checklist of questions that they can work through in pairs. For example:

- Is the language right for a report (or whatever text type is being written)?
- Are the information and the language right for your audience?
- Read your text to your partner. Is there anything that doesn't sound right?
- Have you checked the spelling, punctuation and grammar?

It is often useful to give children a <u>very specific</u> focus for their revising and editing, and then ask them to work on this in pairs. One way the children can do this is to swap texts, and 'mark' their partner's work with some useful suggestions based on the given focus, using a different coloured pen. They then pass back the text, explain their suggestions and work together on improving the text.

It may be helpful to conduct a guided group session for this step with the more able children. They often learn best when spotting weaknesses in their own work and considering a range of possible improvements (see **Guided focus suggestions** on page 9).

Publishing

Conducting a shared publishing session

Time pressures will mean that it is easier to 'publish' some shared texts than others. Where it would be difficult to publish a complete version, pick out instances in the shared text which could benefit from presentational changes.

Remind the children of the intended audience, and any needs or preferences this audience may have. Revise the original purpose for writing, and consider how both of these factors have dictated the form the text has taken. Try to evaluate the impact the text will have on its intended audience.

Discuss the layout of the text. Identify ways in which its presentation could support the content. For instance, clarity of information in a report text could be enhanced through the use of a main title and headings, together with an annotated diagram, or a story could be illustrated in an attractive and informative way. Consider different ways of positioning the illustrations, rather than simply having the text at the top and a picture at the bottom. For example, split the text with the illustration in the middle, or put the text in a column with pictures down the side or decorative borders around the edge.

Discuss briefly the relative merits of highlighting effects such as bold, underlining, italics, enlarged font, changed font, upper case, etc. Decide how to present the title and headings.

Decide on the necessary publication methods and materials. These could include the use of a computer to produce the finished text, or some good handwriting pens and some attractively coloured paper. Using very simple paper-folding techniques, attractive 'books' can be made for the presentation of shorter texts. Despite their simplicity these often encourage children to produce outstanding results.

Publishing in group work

Once again, children can 'echo' the publishing ideas discussed and tried out in the shared session. When the children work on the 'best' copy of their work, it is a good opportunity to consider the importance of clear handwriting and good spelling.

Do everything possible to involve the children in presenting their finished texts to the intended audience, whether this entails them reading their stories to another class, performing their work in school assemblies or producing questionnaires asking other children what they think of work on display in the corridors.

How to plan with *Cornerstones for Writing*

In each year there are six units, corresponding roughly to six half-terms. Each *Cornerstones for Writing* unit takes one text type as its main focus, based on NLS requirements.

It is recommended that each unit be covered over a two-week period of concentrated, writing-focused work, as follows:

Week 1: reading linked to writing;
Week 2: writing.

To accommodate this in the teaching programme, reading and writing objectives for a chosen text type can be <u>blocked</u> together and given a heavier-than-average weighting of teaching time. This can include both literacy hour time and 'other English' time. Most teachers would agree that time beyond the literacy hour is essential in order to fulfil the requirement to teach extended and developed writing. Any remaining NLS writing objectives for each half term are covered in the 'additional sessions' (see below) which follow each unit.

Half term	
Week 1	Work on NLS range of texts
Week 2	for term and (mainly) reading
Week 3	objectives
	Cornerstones for Writing
Week 4	Reading linked to writing
Week 5	Writing
Week 6	As for Weeks 1–3

Each unit leads to the production of developed texts on two levels:

1 by the whole class, done in shared sessions with you, the teacher;
2 by individuals or groups, independently or with your guidance.

Over the course of a unit, you will address and reinforce many text-, sentence- and word-level objectives for the term. Once each unit is under way, particularly in the latter stages of drafting, revising and editing, and publishing, you will probably need to 'flex' the structure of the literacy hour to allow for a 'writing workshop' approach. Whole-class work could be devoted to shared planning or writing, but incorporating supportive sentence- or word-level focuses. Guided support could focus on scaffolding the children's own work as it progresses; independent sessions should allow time for the children to plan, draft and improve their work in the light of what they are learning about the target text type. However, if you wish to follow the classic structure of the literacy hour, a unit could even be followed through in quarter-hour stages, as long as the children's interest is maintained.

It is strongly recommended that plenary sessions be maintained, even where the literacy hour has been 'flexed', in order to sum up and reinforce the children's learning during the course of each writing lesson. In this way, the children discuss not only what they have done, but also how they have done it, and what they have learned about the writing process.

Linking reading and writing objectives

As reading and writing are inextricably linked and mutually supportive, every unit includes close reading analysis of simple model texts. However, it is also strongly recommended that each unit be immediately preceded by further reading experiences within the target text type, in accordance with NLS reading objectives. If, as the children read, they are helped to appreciate how an author has written the text with great care in a particular way and for a particular purpose, it is far more likely that they will be able to write successful texts of their own.

Using the additional sessions

As outlined above, *Cornerstones for Writing* focuses on one main text type per unit (therefore per half term), covering a great many of the writing objectives within the NLS framework. The 'additional sessions' will help you cover the few remaining objectives.

The additional sessions usually consist of a single shared session (or occasionally two or even three sessions) followed by group activities. This is because, assuming that the main text type has been taught in the way we suggest, you will probably plan to give these objectives 'light touch' treatment because of time limitations. However, the content of these sessions varies, and you should use your professional judgement in planning whether/when and how to use the following types of additional session:

- short, one-off tasks which could reasonably be achieved in a single literacy hour session (e.g. **Writing an advert** in unit 6);
- more broadly based objectives which you may wish to expand if time permits (e.g. **Writing a playscript from the story** in unit 1);
- useful skills work which could be slotted into the main two-week writing block if you feel the children are ready for it, or perhaps taught in a guided session to one ability group (e.g. **Making notes** in unit 3).

Special features of *Cornerstones for Writing*

Differentiation by colour coding

In *Cornerstones for Writing*, group follow-up activities are differentiated at three levels. Colour coding is used for this in the pupil's book and referred to in the teaching notes. The following coding is used:

- **red** to indicate activities appropriate for the less able child;
- **blue** to indicate activities appropriate for the average child;
- **yellow** to indicate activities appropriate for the more able child.

Guided focus suggestions (see page 9) are provided in the teacher's book for each session, with different suggestions for each of the red, blue and yellow groups. Additional differentiation can be achieved through the size and constitution of specific groupings. For example, less able or less prolific writers could be supported by allowing them to work collaboratively on one text, in pairs or groups. More able writers could be challenged to produce individual documents.

Guided focus suggestions

Group work allows small groups of children to use for themselves writing skills previously demonstrated and trialled in shared sessions. In guided group work, the demands on children's developing authorship can be carefully structured and focused by the teacher to ensure appropriate differentiation and maximum progress. The teaching notes in this book provide specific suggestions for guided group support at each stage, to help you to achieve this. However, it is of course vital to tailor your focus to the specific needs of the children in each group, which you are in the best position to assess and which no book can fully provide for.

Once writing workshops get under way (see **How to plan with *Cornerstones for Writing*** above) and the emphasis begins to shift from demonstration towards independent writing, you may choose to 'squeeze' the usual half hour of whole-class work down to twenty minutes (the plenary may also be contracted). This creates time for <u>two</u> guided group lessons during each workshop hour, meaning that each group has two teaching visits over the course of a week.

Speaking and listening symbol

Regardless of whether the children carry out their follow-up work individually, in pairs or in groups, it is important that they interact with one another. Specific opportunities for speaking and listening are emphasised in *Cornerstones for Writing* with a special symbol (two talking heads). This appears in the pupil's book next to relevant activities, and is repeated in the summary of activities in the teacher's book.

Structured or focused talk about writing is almost more important than the writing itself because it involves children in <u>thinking about how to write</u> and <u>transmitting ideas</u>. Although teachers sometimes worry that insufficient 'evidence' of writing activity may be produced, the finished texts at the end of each unit should reflect all the teaching and learning that have taken place.

Self-assessment sheets

Cornerstones for Writing encourages children to evaluate their own work and become aware of their progress. A simple self-assessment sheet is provided with each unit, which can be given to each child once they have completed their writing. The sheets may prove suitable for inclusion in records of achievement.

Homework

Many schools now provide regular homework for their pupils, so we include a variety of suggestions at the end of each unit. The suggestions are intended to reinforce the knowledge and skills gained in each unit, though they are not essential to the success of the writing project. To avoid any potential 'paperchase' problems – and to prevent marking overload! – many of the homework suggestions are based on research or involve reading or discussion.

Cross-curricular links

One of the main aims of the NLS is to promote the cross-curricular applications of literacy skills, rather than to teach them as simply 'English'. For instance, if the children are learning how to write reports, a real purpose for report-writing may be found in the science curriculum – the children could present, in a report, all the information they have learnt about materials, life processes, etc. Likewise, children can deploy their recount skills in history lessons, writing 'in role' as eyewitnesses to major events. You should seek cross-curricular links for writing projects wherever possible.

Clear opportunities for cross-curricular links with *Cornerstones for Writing* are highlighted in the teaching notes.

ICT opportunities

ICT will prove particularly valuable in recording, revising and editing class or individual texts. Word-processing offers a quick, easy way of finding and correcting mis-spellings or experimenting with the structure of sentences. Paragraphing, headings and the shape and size of layout can all be changed at the press of a button.

The internet used in researching information is also a powerful tool that can help children plan their writing. Where appropriate, opportunities for using the internet are clearly highlighted in *Cornerstones for Writing*.

Key to symbols

red	activities appropriate for the less able child
blue	activities appropriate for the average child
yellow	activities appropriate for the more able child
	activities appropriate for pair or group work (speaking and listening opportunities)

Note: this section contains facsimiles of OHTs/posters which do not also appear as copymasters.

Historical story — 1

A Camp to Hide King Alfred

Wulfric sat alone in his hideaway on an island in the Somerset marshes. His island was tucked away behind tall reeds and rushes. It could only be reached by a small rowing boat. It was the only place he could go to get away from his younger sister, Eadgifu. He watched the sun setting and thought longingly of becoming a soldier in King Alfred's army.

When Wulfric arrived home it was dark, and his father was angry because he was late. The family were preparing for the Twelfth Night feast. This was Wulfric's favourite feast as a whole pig was spit-roasted. This year was going to be the best one ever, as King Alfred of Wessex had paid the Viking marauders gold to secure peace for his people.

Wulfric sneaked a mouthful of mead from his father's drinking horn. He was enjoying himself. The feast was in full swing when there was a frantic knocking on the door that made the tapestries shake and the candles stutter. In stumbled a youth, his cloak shredded, his hair matted with blood. As he drank a goblet of mead to warm him, he told them the terrible news. "I have ridden for four hours! Chippenham is burned and the King has fled!" A wave of horror swept around the hall. The minstrels stopped singing.

Wulfric's father Aelfwin was master of the hall. He took the youth, Wynflaed, to the bower to speak with him alone, but Wulfric followed them. "The King is in great danger, we must find him a place to hide," Wynflaed whispered urgently.

"I know the very place," said Wulfric as he strode into the bower. They all agreed that Wulfric should show Wynflaed's riding companion, Hereberht, where the place was so he could decide if it was fit for a king.

It was cold, dark and foggy as Wulfric and Hereberht rowed across the water to Wulfric's camp. When they arrived, Hereberht took off his glove and showed Wulfric his ring; it said *Alfred Rex*. He was the King!

When Wulfric arrived home, the first chill light of dawn had already broken through the sky. Wynflaed gave the boy the job of taking food to the King. Later that morning, on the edge of the marsh, he was stopped by Vikings on horseback.

Adapted from *A Camp to Hide King Alfred* by Roy Apps

Historical story — 2

"Where y'going boy?" they demanded. "To my castle," replied Wulfric, and the Vikings guffawed with laughter and rode away.

Over the next few weeks the Vikings searched the villages looking for the King, but eventually they gave up. Meanwhile, Wulfric, his father and the other thanes were visiting the King and preparing for battle against the Vikings.

As the damp greyness of winter gave way to spring, Wulfric knew that the time for revenge was drawing near. At last, the thanes and earls were ready to confront the Vikings, and Wulfric rowed the King back through the bushes towards the village.

"Wulfric," said the King. "I want you to be part of my company when we march on the Vikings." Wulfric felt this was the most exciting day of his whole life, but his father disagreed – "He's only a boy, sire!" So it was decided that Wulfric should stay at home.

That afternoon, Wulfric sat at the edge of the courtyard, watching the men load horses and wagons for the long march against the Vikings. He looked up and saw Eadgifu. "Go, Wulfric," she urged, "I'll explain to mother. Go on, big brother!" So Wulfric slipped under the covers of a large wagon and stowed away to fight for his king.

In the seventh week after Easter, Wulfric rode with his king against the Viking army at Edington. The fighting was fierce. Wulfric's helmet weighed on his head and his sword grew heavy in his hand, but in the end, the Vikings fled.

For two weeks, Alfred's army laid siege to the Viking camp, then on the fourteenth day a solitary figure tramped wearily out of the Viking camp towards Alfred's tent. It was Guthrum, the Viking King.

"Alfred, King of the people of Wessex. We have no wood to burn, no food to eat. I come to make peace, on your terms."

The peace was made. Guthrum and his Vikings withdrew from Wessex. Alfred's soldiers made their way home, but Wulfric decided to stay and serve his king. They rode together towards Wessex's southern coast and stopped on the top of a hill, looking down at the English Channel, glistening in the afternoon sunlight.

"Would you be prepared to sail a boat as one of my first sea soldiers, Wulfric?" King Alfred asked.

Wulfric thought of the days he had spent in his camp, dreaming of the sea, and could think of no better thing.

Adapted from *A Camp to Hide King Alfred* by Roy Apps

Note: this section contains facsimiles of OHTs/posters which do not also appear as copymasters.

From *King Arthur*

Arthur was a squire. That meant he could wear a short sword at his belt and dress in fine clothes on special occasions, but it also meant that he was at the beck and call of his older brother, Kay. Kay was already a knight and should have known better, but he seemed to enjoy ordering Arthur about. He even made Arthur empty out his bath water and groom his horse, treating him more like a servant than a squire and brother.

From *Beowulf*

"Stranger!" called Hygelac.

The men near the King stopped talking and picking their teeth and swilling stone-cold mead over their gums.

"Stranger," called Hygelac.

In the hall of the Geats a hundred men listened.

"Your name?" demanded Hygelac.

"Gangleri," said the stranger. "In your tongue: *Wanderer*."

"All right, Wanderer. It's time you sang for your supper."

Men on the mead benches shifted their buttocks, and stretched out their legs. The gathering faced inwards towards the fire.

Wanderer stood in the poet's place by the hearth and rubbed his one gleaming eye. "I'll fuel you," he said, "with a true story, and one close to my heart. This story of past, present and future."

"True?" called out a young man, the King's nephew, Beowulf by name. "How can it be true if it is in the future?"

"Because it is not finished," said Wanderer. "You must finish it."

From *The Last of the Vikings*

At Stiklestad six spears came at Harald, swift as snakes, rattling against each other, ash against ash, in haste to end him. He stumbled on the churned up turf and fell, the spear shafts criss-crossing over him like the roof beams of a house, their iron points in the ground on either side of his body.

An unexpected visitor

Ryan sat in his den at the bottom of the park. It was the only place he could go to get away from his sister Chantelle. It was here that he watched the sun setting, as he aimed stones at empty Coke cans, ate crisps and chocolate and thought longingly of going into the British army.

When Ryan got home it was dark, and his father was angry because he was late. All the family was busy preparing for a New Year's Eve party, which was going to be the best one ever. It was the start of a new millennium – the Year 2000!

The party was in full swing. Ryan sneaked a mouthful of lager from his father's can.

Suddenly there was a frantic ringing on the doorbell, which made the photographs shake and the light bulbs tremble. In stumbled a youth, his tracksuit shredded, his hair matted with blood. Everyone stood around the mysterious stranger. The stereo was switched off, food and bottles of wine lay untouched on the table.

Note: this section contains facsimiles of OHTs/posters which do not also appear as copymasters.

8

Newspaper-style recount

CAT-NAPPING KITTEN GETS CARRIED AWAY

Four-hundred-mile journey uses up one of the nine lives of lucky Megan

A stray kitten that curled up for a nap inside the bonnet of a brand-new car was taken 400 miles from Scotland to the south of England before being discovered.

The kitten's ordeal began at a Glasgow car dealer's. She found shelter and warmth on the engine of a family saloon. Then someone bought the car and drove it away. They had no idea that there was an extra passenger.

Luckily Megan stayed still throughout her journey and it was not until the new owner lifted the bonnet to admire his new engine that she was finally found.

Her black-and-white fur was infested with fleas, mites and lice, so although the journey did not harm her, she was shocked, in very poor condition,

underfed and much in need of care.

Anne Rowan at the Blue Cross Animal Sanctuary in Chalfont St Peter, Buckinghamshire, says: "Megan is feeling much better now. She will soon be off to the new home that we have found for her."

© Cambridge University Press 2001

7

Historical story

Badgers

Badgers come creeping from dark underground,
Badgers scratch hard with a bristly sound,
Badgers go nosing around.

Badgers have whiskers and black and white faces,
Badger cubs scramble and scrap and run races,
Badgers like overgrown places.

Badgers don't jump when a vixen screams,
Badgers drink quietly from moonshiny streams,
Badgers dig holes in our dreams.

Badgers are working while you and I sleep,
Pushing their tunnels down twisting and steep,
Badgers have secrets to keep.

'Badgers' by Richard Edwards

© Cambridge University Press 2001

Note: this section contains facsimiles of OHTs/posters which do not also appear as copymasters.

10

Pupils skip to **£2,000** cash boost

Roped in... Milton Road Junior School pupils skip to it

Who?	What?	Where?
When?	Why?	How?

9

Earthquake in Japan

FANGS A LOT!

BATTLE OF THE BURGER

QUEEN to visit Australia

Fans storm pitch

Shell-shocked

In search of home waters... The turtle which needs a home, pictured with RSPCA inspector, Chris Nice

Note: this section contains facsimiles of OHTs/posters which do not also appear as copymasters.

13

HOW TO GET TO MY HOUSE FROM SCHOOL

How to find my road
Come out of the school gates. Turn right.

Walk to the corner.

The entrance to the park is on your left.

Follow the path that goes straight ahead.

Go through the gate.

Turn left.

Take the first road on the right.

You have found my road. Now you have to find my house.

How to find my house
You will see a narrow alley on your right.

There is a small square of grass.

I used to play there when I was very small.

Look for the green door.

Look for the number 22.

Ring the bell and I will let you in.

You will be very welcome.

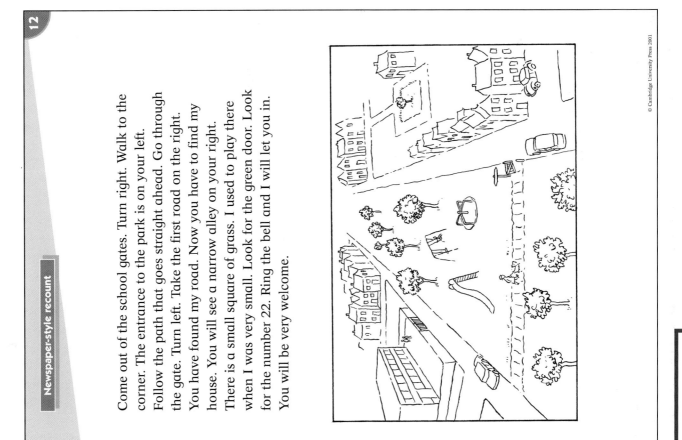

12

Come out of the school gates. Turn right. Walk to the corner. The entrance to the park is on your left. Follow the path that goes straight ahead. Go through the gate. Turn left. Take the first road on the right. You have found my road. Now you have to find my house. You will see a narrow alley on your right. There is a small square of grass. I used to play there when I was very small. Look for the green door. Look for the number 22. Ring the bell and I will let you in. You will be very welcome.

Note: this section contains facsimiles of OHTs/posters which do not also appear as copymasters.

Poem about an imagined world

The Dong with a Luminous Nose

Long years ago
The Dong was happy and gay,
Till he fell in love with a Jumbly Girl
Who came to those shores one day,
For the Jumblies came in a sieve, they did, –
Landing at eve near the Zemmery Fidd
Where the Oblong Oysters grow,
And the rocks are smooth and grey.
And all the woods and the valleys rang
With the Chorus they daily and nightly sang, –
    "Far and few, far and few,
Are the lands where the Jumblies live;
Their heads are green, and their hands are blue,
    And they went to sea in a sieve."

Happily, happily passed those days!
While the cheerful Jumblies stayed;
They danced in circlets all night long,
To the plaintive pipe of the lively Dong,
    In moonlight, shine, or shade.
For day and night he was always there
By the side of the Jumbly Girl so fair,
With her sky-blue hands and her sea-green hair.
Till the morning came of that hateful day
When the Jumblies sailed in their sieve away,
And the Dong was left on the cruel shore
    Gazing – gazing for evermore, –
    Ever keeping his weary eyes on
That pea-green sail on the far horizon, –
    Singing the Jumbly Chorus still
As he sate all day on the grassy hill, –
    "Far and few, far and few,
Are the lands where the Jumblies live;
Their heads are green, and their hands are blue,
    And they went to sea in a sieve."

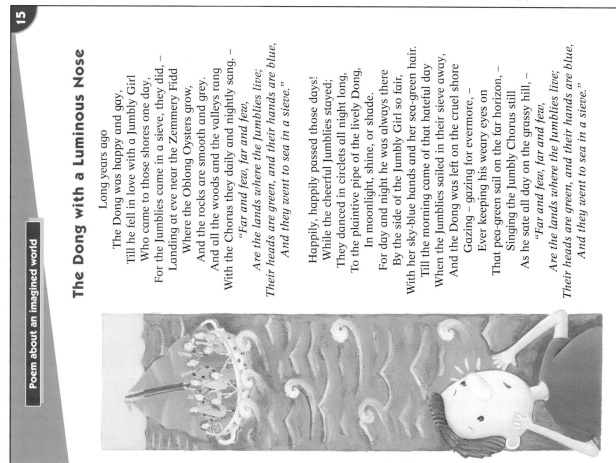

Poem about an imagined world

The King of Quizzical Island

The King of Quizzical Island
Had a most inquisitive mind.
He said, "If I sail to the edge of the world
I wonder what I'll find?"

So he sailed up the Jigsaw River
And there, round the final bend,
He found himself in Vertical Land
Where everything stands on end.

The rivers go up like fountains
And the crocodiles stand on their tails
And the meadows tower like mountains
And the trains run on vertical rails.

The King said "That's one way of using
Every inch of space that you've got –
But it doesn't look very comfortable...."
And the crocodiles said, "It's not!"

So the singular ship sailed upwards
On a river tall and wide
And from the top of the river
It sailed down the other side.

Note: this section contains facsimiles of OHTs/posters which do not also appear as copymasters.

Poem about an imagined world

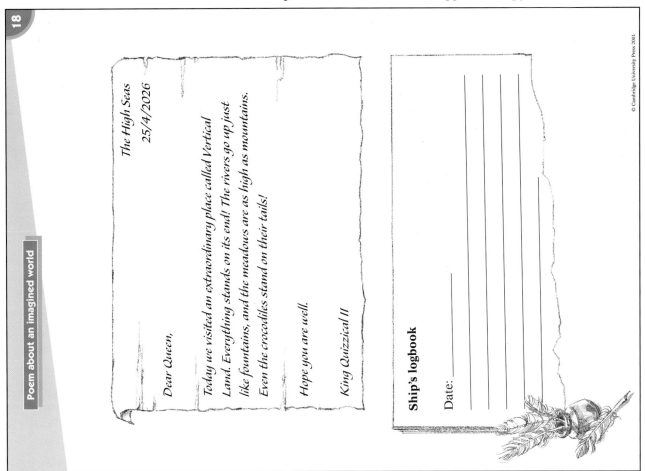

The High Seas
25/4/2026

Dear Queen,

Today we visited an extraordinary place called Vertical Land. Everything stands on its end! The rivers go up just like fountains, and the meadows are as high as mountains. Even the crocodiles stand on their tails!

Hope you are well.

King Quizzical II

Ship's logbook

Date: _____

Poem about an imagined world

Jabberwocky

"Twas brillig, and the slithy toves
Did gyre and gimble in the wabe:
All mimsy were the borogoves,
And the mome raths outgrabe.

"Beware the Jabberwock, my son!
The jaws that bite, the claws that catch!
Beware the Jubjub bird, and shun
The frumious Bandersnatch!"

He took his vorpal sword in hand:
Long time the manxome foe he sought –
So rested he by the Tumtum tree,
And stood awhile in thought.

And, as in uffish thought he stood,
The Jabberwock, with eyes of flame,
Came whiffling through the tulgey wood,
And burbled as it came!

One, two! One, two! And through and through
The vorpal blade went snicker-snack!
He left it dead, and with its head
He went galumphing back.

"And, hast thou slain the Jabberwock?
Come to my arms, my beamish boy!
Oh frabjous day! Callooh! Callay!"
He chortled in his joy.

"Twas brillig, and the slithy toves
Did gyre and gimble in the wabe;
All mimsy were the borogoves,
And the mome raths outgrabe.

18

Note: this section contains facsimiles of OHTs/posters which do not also appear as copymasters.

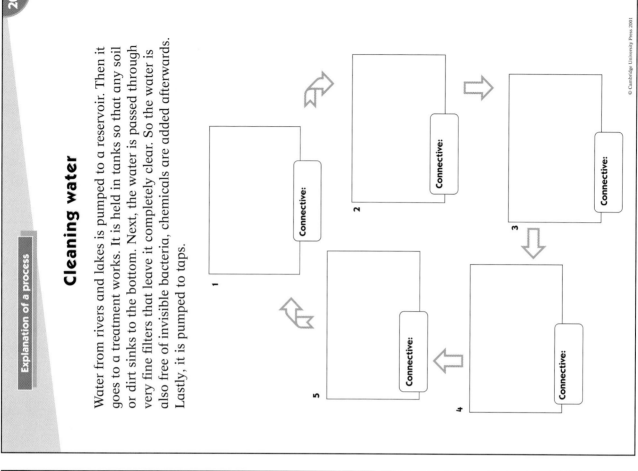

20

Cleaning water

Water from rivers and lakes is pumped to a reservoir. Then it goes to a treatment works. It is held in tanks so that any soil or dirt sinks to the bottom. Next, the water is passed through very fine filters that leave it completely clear. So the water is also free of invisible bacteria, chemicals are added afterwards. Lastly, it is pumped to taps.

1   Connective:

2   Connective:

3   Connective:

4   Connective:

5   Connective:

© Cambridge University Press 2001

19

Explanation of a process

Cleaning water

The importance of clean water
Water is essential for life. It is needed for drinking, as well as washing, cooking and many industrial processes. After it is used, however, water is often dirty and contaminated. For this reason, the process of cleaning water is very important.

Making fresh water clean enough to drink
Water from rivers and lakes is pumped to a reservoir. Then it goes to a treatment works. It is held in tanks so that any soil or dirt sinks to the bottom. Next, the water is passed through very fine filters that leave it completely clear. So that the water is also free of invisible bacteria, chemicals are added afterwards. Lastly, it is pumped to taps.

Cleaning up used water
When it is flushed away, dirty water is carried along a drainage system to a sewage works. Immediately, paper, plastic and other materials are sieved out. Then the sewage is held in settlement tanks so that solid matter settles as sludge, and can be taken out. The remaining liquid is passed through filters in order to remove pollution. Finally, the water is clean enough to release back into rivers and seas.

The importance of recycling water
The Earth's water is very old and is constantly recycled by natural processes. However, this planetary hydrological cycle cannot cope with the high levels of water pollution produced by humans. Governments are introducing environmental protection laws, which demand efficient water-cleaning processes to protect the planet's water.

© Cambridge University Press 2001

Note: this section contains facsimiles of OHTs/posters which do not also appear as copymasters.

23

NOTES ON WOOL-MAKING

Wool = fibres from fleece of sheep
Sheep farmed for wool
½ world's wool from Australia
and N.Z.

Spring - heavy winter fleece
shaved (shearing)
Fleece to woollen mill

Fibres - separated different
lengths
Washed to remove grease/dirt +
straightened out
Fed through machine + combed
into soft, thin layer (web)

22

Wool-making

Most wool is made from short *fibres* that come from the *fleece* of a sheep. Sheep are farmed specially for the wool they produce. Nearly half the world's wool comes from Australia and New Zealand.

Each spring, the sheep's heavy winter fleece is shaved off. This is called *shearing*. The fleece is then taken to a woollen mill.

At the mill, fibres from the fleece are separated into different lengths, then washed to remove grease and dirt. After washing, the fibres are straightened out. They are fed through a machine that combs them together into a soft, thin layer called a *web*. This process is known as *carding*.

Next, the web is split into thin strands. These are twisted together into long threads by a spinning machine. The strands are spun several times, getting thinner and stronger each time.

After spinning, the wool can be *knitted* into jumpers or *woven* into cloth. Wool is a good material for clothes because it is strong and warm, and keeps its shape even when stretched.

Note: this section contains facsimiles of OHTs/posters which do not also appear as copymasters.

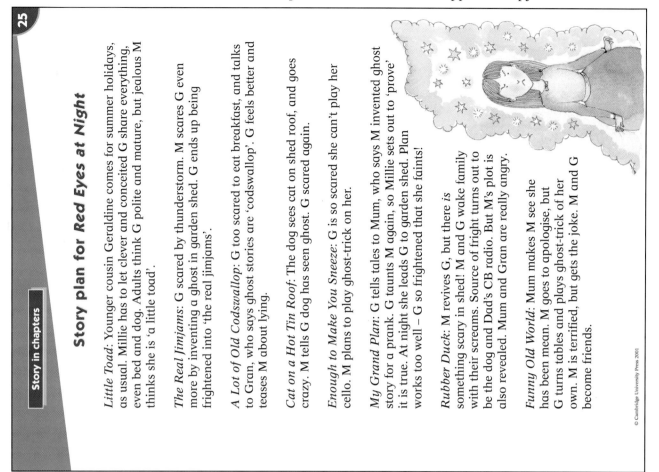

Story in chapters

Story plan for *Red Eyes at Night*

Little Toad: Younger cousin Geraldine comes for summer holidays, as usual. Millie has to let clever and conceited G share everything, even bed and dog. Adults think G polite and mature, but jealous M thinks she is 'a little toad'.

The Real Jimjams: G scared by thunderstorm. M scares G even more by inventing a ghost in garden shed. G ends up being frightened into 'the real jimjams'.

A Lot of Old Codswallop: G too scared to eat breakfast, and talks to Gran, who says ghost stories are 'codswallop'. G feels better and teases M about lying.

Cat on a Hot Tin Roof: The dog sees cat on shed roof, and goes crazy. M tells G dog has seen ghost. G scared again.

Enough to Make You Sneeze: G is so scared she can't play her cello. M plans to play ghost-trick on her.

My Grand Plan: G tells tales to Mum, who says M invented ghost story for a prank. G taunts M again, so Millie sets out to 'prove' it is true. At night she leads G to garden shed. Plan works too well – G so frightened that she faints!

Rubber Duck: M revives G, but there *is* something scary in shed! M and G wake family with their screams. Source of fright turns out to be the dog and Dad's CB radio. But M's plot is also revealed. Mum and Gran are really angry.

Funny Old World: Mum makes M see she has been mean. M goes to apologise, but G turns tables and plays ghost-trick of her own. M is terrified, but gets the joke. M and G become friends.

© Cambridge University Press 2001

Story in chapters

R E D   E Y E S   A T   N I G H T

From *Red Eyes at Night* by Michael Morpurgo

© Cambridge University Press 2001

Note: this section contains facsimiles of OHTs/posters which do not also appear as copymasters.

28

Persuasive writing

Save trees – waste less paper!

We waste too much paper at school. We must cut down on the amount of paper that we use. In the United Kingdom, over 6 million tonnes of paper and card is thrown away every year. This means that more trees have to be cut down to make new paper. Therefore, we need to try to reduce this waste in every way that we can.

Every day, our bins are full of discarded paper and card. A lot of this paper could have been saved because there is still empty space that could be used. We should use every bit of space on the paper. It is also important to reuse paper for scrap or rough work. Many children bring cartons of drink to school. This also wastes paper because cartons can only be used once and then have to be thrown away. Flasks, however, can be used again and again. Therefore, if children brought drinks in flasks then we would cut down on waste. Finally, the school should send our waste paper to a recycling bin and also buy recycled paper. If we did all these things then the school would buy less paper every year.

There are many ways that we can save paper at school. It is important to do this if we are to save more trees from being destroyed. It is up to all of us to stop the waste!

© Cambridge University Press 2001

27

Story in chapters

Haiku Moment

Stopped here listening –
this heedless grind of traffic
staggers the birdsongs.

There was an Old Man in a Tree

There was an Old Man in a tree,
Whose whiskers were lovely to see;
But the birds of the air
Pluck'd them perfectly bare,
To make themselves nests in that tree.

Night Mail

This is the Night Mail crossing the Border,
Bringing the cheque and the postal order,

Letters for the rich, letters for the poor,
The shop at the corner, the girl next door.

Pulling up Beattock, a steady climb:
The gradient's against her, but she's on time.

Past cotton-grass and moorland boulder,
Shovelling white steam over her shoulder,

Snorting noisily, she passes
Silent miles of wind-bent grasses.

'Haiku Moment' by James Berry; 'There was an Old Man in a Tree' by Edward Lear; From 'Night Mail' by W. H. Auden

© Cambridge University Press 2001

Note: this section contains facsimiles of OHTs/posters which do not also appear as copymasters.

22

30

Persuasive writing

Sunnydale Primary School
Birmingham B17 0ZN

Friday, 1st June 2001

Dear Mr Peters

We think that there is not enough to do at playtime and that the playground equipment needs improving. At the moment, there is nothing in the playground except a faded hopscotch grid so most children are bored when they are outside.

More playground equipment would improve behaviour at playtime. There are several reasons why we think this: children would be busy playing instead of getting into arguments, children would not keep trying to sneak indoors and they would not try to bring toys secretly in their pockets to play with. Climbing frames and balancing beams would also be good for our health because we would be exercising and getting fit.

If we had new playground equipment we would look forward to coming to school because playtime would be so much fun. Our playground needs improving. Please consider our proposal.

Yours sincerely

Year 4

© Cambridge University Press 2001

29

Persuasive writing

Pet care

Many animals that are given as pets are not looked after properly. This is often because their owner forgets to feed them or does not think about the need to keep the animal clean. Pets need the right amount of food at a regular time in the day. They have to be clean and also need somewhere clean to live. It is important that they are handled correctly, and given due care and attention. If any of these needs is not met then pets can become ill, lonely and frightened. Children can sometimes be quite rough when handling animals so the pet can be frightened. If the pet is held wrongly or dropped then it may become nervous and even bite or scratch. In some cases, pets are simply abandoned because their owner no longer wants to look after them.

© Cambridge University Press 2001

Note: this section contains facsimiles of OHTs/posters which do not also appear as copymasters.

31

Persuasive writing

The Demon Domestic

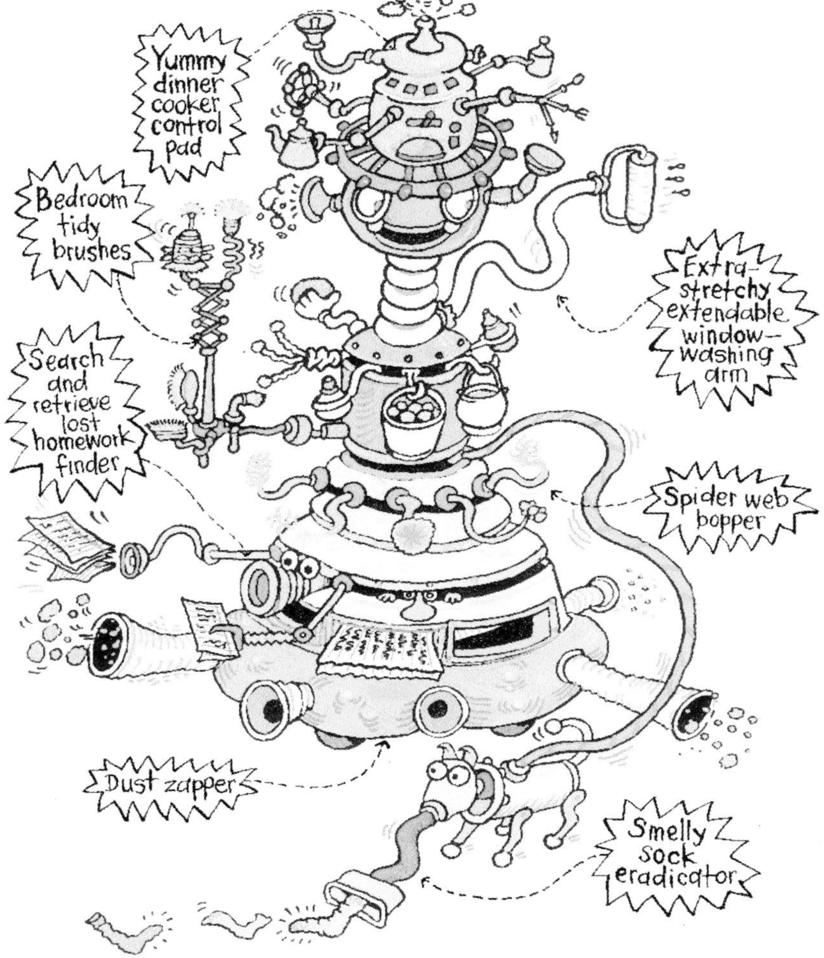

32

Persuasive writing

From *Charlie and the Chocolate Factory*

"My dear sir!" cried Mr Wonka, "when I start selling this gum in the shops it will change *everything*! It will be the end of all kitchens and cooking! There will be no more shopping to do! No more buying of meat and groceries! There'll be no knives and forks at mealtimes! No plates! No washing up! No rubbish! No mess! Just a little strip of Wonka's magic chewing gum – and that's all you'll ever need at breakfast, lunch and supper! This piece of gum I've just made happens to be tomato soup, roast beef and blueberry pie, but you can have almost anything you want!"

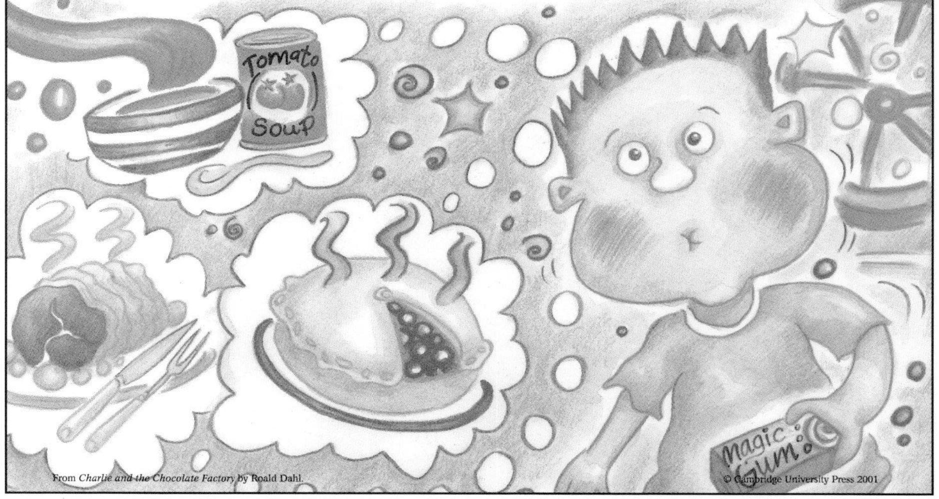

From *Charlie and the Chocolate Factory* by Roald Dahl.

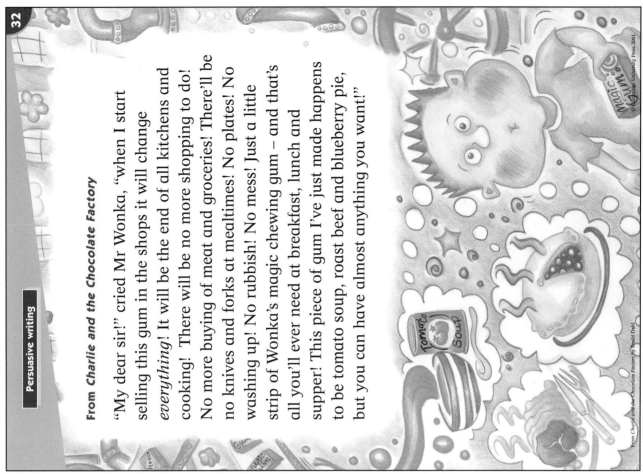

Term one fiction focus:
1 How to write a historical story

What most children will already know:

The narrative structure of a story – beginning, middle and end

That the beginning of the story sets the scene and introduces the characters

That stories contain problems and resolutions

The importance of chronological order

How to plan a simple story

How to write dialogue in a story

What children will learn in this unit:

How to set a story in the past

How to develop characters

How to develop the middle section of a story

How to develop the use of chronology in a story

Different ways of planning a story

---

1 Looking at the story structure

Objectives

It will save time if you read 'A Camp to Hide King Alfred' on OHTs/posters 1 and 2 in advance of this session.

To understand the structure of a story (introduction, build up, climax/conflict, resolution) and to use this to develop a frame for children's own writing

To understand that the middle of a story contains several events which lead to a climax of conflict before the resolution

Shared session

You need: OHTs/posters 1 and 2, OHT/poster 3.

1 This story has an Anglo-Saxon setting, but it could also be used when studying Vikings (the cross-curricular link is with the 'Invaders and settlers' history units).

2 The steps involved in writing a historical story are the same for whichever historical period you study in Year 4. However, it may be helpful to begin from a shared text which has specific reference to the period you have worked on with your children in history.

3 It is strongly recommended that this writing unit is done at the end of a unit of study in history so that the children have the background knowledge they will need to undertake the writing of a historical story.

- Explain that over the next two weeks you are going to learn how to write a historical story. This is a story which is set in the past. These stories can involve made-up characters, but to write them, the children need a lot of information about a historical period.

- Tell children that today they are going to find out more about how to organise a story. Ask them what they already know about how a story is structured (e.g. beginning, middle, end). If necessary, read *A Camp to Hide King Alfred*.

- With children, identify and draw boxes round the beginning, middle and end sections on OHTs/posters 1 and 2 (e.g. beginning: up to *swept around the hall*; end: from *For two weeks, Alfred's army...*).

- Explain that this story has a simple structure, but the author had a more detailed plan of what he was going to write before he started his book. You are going to work together as 'story detectives' to find out what that plan was.

- Recap what is in the beginning of a story (i.e. setting, characters, a problem). Look at the beginning of this story. Identify and underline these elements.

- Look at the end of the story. Identify and underline the solution to the problem set at the beginning of the story. Revise the term for this – the **resolution**.

- Use OHT/poster 3. Ignore the time headings for this session – you will use them in Session 2. Write planning notes for the beginning and ending (see the example below).

■ Now consider the middle of the story. Elicit the main events from the children and write these on the planning sheet.

■ Identify with the children the main event of the middle of the story (Wulfric and the Saxon army fighting the Vikings). Introduce the word **climax**. Show the children that the events in the middle of the story lead up to this main event, and that it can sometimes be a conflict, as it is here. Remind the children that this is a historical story, so the main event is based in fact – there really was a siege at Edington.

■ Write planning notes for the middle section. Your completed story plan should look similar to this:

BEGINNING	MIDDLE	END
Characters: Wulfric (Saxon boy) Setting: Island in Somerset marshes; Saxon hall Problem: Vikings attack Saxons	King needs place to hide – Wulfric offers his hideout Wulfric takes King to his hiding place Wulfric takes food to King – meets Vikings Vikings search for King Wulfric brings King back to village Wulfric stows away and follows Alfred into battle *Climax*: Wulfric and Saxon army fight Vikings	*Resolution*: Vikings defeated Wulfric becomes sea soldier

■ Explain that this is probably what the author's plan of his story looked like before he wrote the full version.

Group follow-up activities

A listening centre would be useful for all these activities. Children could record their stories, and play them back, identifying each section of the story as they listen.

1 red   Pupil's book page 4

Children reorganise a simplified version of the model text and draw boxes around the beginning, middle and end sections. They then tell the story to their partner.

Guided group support   Reinforce children's knowledge of story structure. Encourage them to use as much description as possible when telling the story to their partner.

2 blue   Pupil's book page 5   copymaster 1

Children read another historical story, divided into beginning, middle and end sections. They use copymaster 1 to write planning notes for the story.

Guided group support   Help children understand that the climax is the <u>most dramatic event</u> in the middle part of the story – other events lead up to it, but it is not necessarily the last event before the resolution. (The climax in this story occurs when the slave-woman leaves the baby on the mountain. This is followed by a further event when the dog refuses to follow the slave-woman.)

3 yellow   Pupil's book page 6

Children are given the plan of the beginning and end of a historical story. They have to plan the middle section, including a climax. They then take it in turns to tell the story to a partner.

Guided group support   Make the point about the climax, as with the blue group. Encourage children to plan several events for the middle of their stories.

Plenary Look at some of the children's story plans and use them to reinforce the concept of story structure. Display the shared work you have done. This will serve as useful reference material when children write their own stories, as well as showing the development of the story-writing process.

② Showing the passing of time in a story

Objectives To develop the use of chronology in writing stories

To understand how time passes in stories: through the language of time; through events

Shared session *You need: OHTs/posters 1 and 2, OHT/poster 3 (from Session 1), a large sheet of paper for class poster.*

- Explain that you are going to learn how to show time passing in stories.

- Ask how much time children think passed between Wulfric sitting in his hideout at the beginning of the story and his becoming one of Alfred's sea soldiers at the end. Accept all answers, then explain to children that they are going to be 'time detectives', and try to find out the answer from the story.

- Read the story again. Ask children to identify the words and phrases that tell us about the passing of time. Use your saved OHT/poster 3 from Session 1, and write these words under the time headings for each section of the story.

- Discuss with children that much of what we know about the chronology of the story is <u>deduced</u> from what we are told – this is why we need to be detectives when we are reading. For example, the story does not state that *it was dusk*. Instead, the author has written *he watched the sun setting*, and from this we can deduce that the story starts in the evening. This is a good way of developing vocabulary.

- Your completed time-plan may look like this:

Story	Time
Beginning	
Wulfric alone in his hideaway in the marshes	dusk (*sun setting*)
Goes home for the Twelfth Night feast	evening (*it was dark*) 6th January (*Twelfth Night feast*)
Vikings attack the Saxons	afternoon (four hours ride)

Middle	
King needs a place to hide – Wulfric offers his hideout	later in the evening (*the feast was in full swing*)
Wulfric takes King to his hiding place	night time (*it was cold, dark and foggy*)
Wulfric takes food to King – meets the Vikings	morning (*Later that morning*)
Vikings search for King	weeks (*over the next few weeks*)
Wulfric brings King back to village	spring (*as the damp greyness of winter gave way to spring*)
Wulfric hides away and follows Alfred	afternoon (*that afternoon*)
Conflict/Climax Wulfric and Saxon army fight the Vikings	May/June (*in the seventh week after Easter*)
End *Resolution* Vikings defeated	two weeks later (*on the fourteenth day*)
Wulfric becomes sea soldier	afternoon (*glistening in the afternoon sunlight*)

- Work out with children how long the story took (about six months – from 6th January until approximately the middle of June).

- Mark on the time-plan how much of the story takes place in one night (the beginning and half the middle of the story). Point out that we are given lots of details about what happens in one night, then weeks go past. Ask children why they think this is (e.g. we are given details about important/main events, but other events are skimmed over because they are not essential to the plot).

- Explain that time phrases are very useful when children are writing their own stories, and as they can see in the story, they are often a good way to start a sentence. Children will need to choose carefully which time phrases to use when they are writing their own story as some describe time in minutes, others in years.

Group follow-up activities

1 red   Pupil's book page 7   copymaster 2

Children read the time phrases in the pupil's book, and put them into the correct 'time' box on copymaster 2.

Guided group support   Focus on children's understanding of the meaning of time phrases.

2 blue/yellow   Pupil's book page 7   copymaster 2

Children read the time phrases from *A Camp to Hide King Alfred* in the pupil's book, and put them into the correct box on copymaster 2. They then go on to add phrases of their own – ask for one per box for the blue group; two for the yellow group.

Guided group support
Blue As with the red group, helping children to understand the different time-spans the time phrases describe. If there is time, ask children to pick out the time phrases from *The Saga of Leif Erikson* on page 5 of the pupil's book, and put them in the correct boxes on copymaster 2.
Yellow Help children develop confidence in thinking of alternative words and phrases. Encourage the use of a thesaurus for this task.

Plenary Ask children to contribute time phrases from their various group activities, and write these up on a poster to create a word bank of time words. Keep this to refer to in subsequent writing sessions.

③ How to set your story in a historical period

Objectives To understand how an author sets a story in the past

To identify details in story settings, and how these affect the reader

To compile a historical word bank to use in story writing

Shared session *You need: OHT/poster 4, OHT/poster 1, a large sheet of paper for class poster.*

- Tell children that they are going to find out how to set a story in a historical period. To do this, they are first going to look at the beginning of another story.

- Read the modern-day story beginning on OHT/poster 4.

- Ask children when the story is set and how they know this. Ask them to identify and underline the **setting** (objects and places) and **characters** which give them clues to the period of the story (e.g. *Ryan, den, park, Chantelle, Coke cans, crisps, chocolate, British army, Year 2000, lager, can, doorbell, photographs, light bulbs, tracksuit, disco, bottles of wine*).

- Now read the beginning of *A Camp to Hide King Alfred* again. As before, ask children to identify and underline specific vocabulary which gives clues to the historical period (e.g. *Wulfric, Eadgifu, whole pig spit-roasted, King Alfred of Wessex, Viking marauders, King has fled, mead, drinking horn, goblet, cloak, tapestries, candles, minstrels*).

- On a Saxon word bank poster, list the vocabulary under three headings:

Setting	Characters	Actions and objects
Twelfth Night feast	Wulfric	whole pig spit-roasted
Viking marauders	Eadgifu	mead
Vikings attack	King Alfred	drinking horn
Chippenham	minstrels	cloak
King has fled		candles
		tapestries

- Explain to children that they are going to need lots of factual information about the historical period to write a story which their readers will <u>believe</u> is set in the past. This 'Saxon' word bank will help children with their stories, as well as their activities in this session.

Group follow-up activities

Children will need some knowledge of the period if they choose to describe the Saxon village. It would be useful for them to have access to relevant non-fiction books for this session.

1 red   Pupil's book page 8

Children look at a picture of a Saxon hall like the one in the story. They write down the objects and people they can see, as well as the smells and sounds they can imagine.

Guided group support   Support children in using the class word bank as well as other resources (relevant non-fiction books, dictionaries, a thesaurus).

2 blue   Pupil's book page 9

Children use either the picture of the Saxon hall or of a Saxon village. They write a straightforward description of what they see, smell and hear.

Guided group support   As with the red group. Support children in using full sentences, correctly punctuated.

3 yellow   Pupil's book page 9

Children choose either of the pictures. They imagine that they are tour guides showing a group of visitors around a Saxon hall or village. They write the 'script' for the tour guide.

Guided group support   Encourage children to use descriptive language and specific vocabulary (use the resources suggested for the red group). Ask children to give their village a name – point out that lots of place names date from Saxon times.

Alternative group activity   red

One child describes the scene, while their partner draws it. They then swap roles and, finally, compare their pictures with the one in the book.

Plenary   Use children's research to continue the 'Saxon' word bank poster which you started in the shared session. Alternatively, ask volunteers to read out their descriptions. The rest of the class listens for words and phrases which indicate that these are historical settings. They should also listen for any modern words which sound out of place.

4 How to create characters for your story

Objectives   To identify the characteristics of the main character, using the text to justify views

To use this knowledge to create characters

Shared session   *You need: OHTs/posters 1 and 2, OHT/poster 5, name-badges and/or cloak (see below).*

- Tell children they are going to create characters for their stories. Explain that in a historical story you may have characters who really lived (such as King Alfred) but the main character is often fictitious (such as Wulfric).

- Tell children that they are going to be newspaper reporters for the *Anglo-Saxon Times*. They have heard about Wulfric's adventures, and they are going to interview him for the paper. However, before they do this, they need to find out about what he is like.

- Use the character profile framework on OHT/poster 5, as well as *A Camp to Hide King Alfred* on poster or OHT. Ask children to help you fill in the character profile for Wulfric, using evidence from the text. Highlight the parts of the text which support children's ideas – for example:

Wulfric's age. His father tells the King that he is only a boy and the Vikings call him a boy, but he goes to fight in the army. He can't be <u>very</u> young – *possibly 13 or 14.* There are no right or wrong answers for this, just sensible estimates.

Wulfric's personality. We can tell he is *clever*, because he knows that his hideaway will be a good place to hide the King. He tells the Vikings he is going *to my castle*, which lets them think that he is just a boy pretending to have a castle. However, the hideaway really has become a castle, as the King is living there. We also know Wulfric is *naughty*, because he is late home, and drinks some mead when his father is not looking.

■ Explain that much of the information needed for the character profile is not given directly in the story. Children have to be detectives and work it out from clues in the text.

■ When you have filled in the character profile, tell children that they are now going to interview Wulfric for the newspaper. Give them ten minutes to work in pairs/groups to write some questions to ask him.

■ Choose a volunteer to sit in the 'hot-seat' as Wulfric. Bring in a prop (possibly a cloak) or name-badge for the volunteer to wear – this makes it easier to take on the persona of the character. If you have no willing or able volunteers, try being Wulfric yourself!

■ Use OHT/poster 5 again. Ask children to think of a character for the historical story you will write together. They need to decide whether this character will be a boy or a girl, as well as details about age, family, appearance and interests. Fill these in on the framework.

■ Ask children to decide what kind of personality this character is going to have. Is he/she brave or scared (or both!), naughty or obedient? Do you want the reader to like or dislike your character – are they going to be a 'goody' or a 'baddy'? Write this on the framework.

■ Ask how you will show the character's personality in their actions and the things they say in the story. Again, write this on the framework.

■ Tell children they are now going to write a profile for the main character in their own story. They can use the space on the back of the profile to make notes about any other characters whom they wish to include in their story.

Group follow-up activities

1 red   Pupil's book page 10   copymaster 3

Children create characters for their stories. They look at the Saxon boy and girl pictured in the pupil's book, and use the detailed framework on copymaster 3 to write a character profile. They exchange profiles with a partner, and ask and answer questions about each other's characters.

Guided group support   Help children to use the vocabulary in the profile to write simple sentences about their characters.

2 blue/yellow   Pupil's book page 11

As for activity 1, but using the framework in the pupil's book.

Guided group support

Blue Encourage children to include details about their characters which will affect the reader. Look at examples from the model text where the reader feels sorry for Wulfric (e.g. he escapes from his younger sister; he is told he cannot go to war).

Yellow As with the blue group. Challenge children to think about how they will convey their characters' personalities in actions and in speech.

Alternative group activity   **red/blue/yellow**

Children may wish to create their own characters, and not use the pictures in the book. They can draw their own character and write a description of him/her.

Plenary   Ask volunteers to read out the profiles they have written for their characters. Those listening think of questions they would like to ask the characters. The volunteers then sit in the 'hot-seat' as their characters, to answer these questions.

(5) Planning the story

Objectives   To establish an audience for the class story and for children's own stories

To learn how to plan a historical story using the framework from the model text

Shared session   *You need: OHT/poster 3, 'Time' word bank poster (from Session 2), OHT/poster 5 (from Session 4).*

■ Recap on the character the class created in Session 4. Explain to children that, in their shared work as well as on their own, they are going to make up a story about their fictitious characters, using a historical event to provide the background. This event may influence the ending of the story (e.g. winning a battle can provide a happy ending; losing a battle may mean a sad ending).

■ Establish the audience for the story (e.g. writing for a parallel class; for older children who have studied this period of history; for younger children, to teach them about the historical period through the story).

■ Now brainstorm some of the main events in your chosen historical period. Some ideas for Saxon times are:

- 878 – Alfred fights the Vikings at Edington (backdrop to *A Camp to Hide King Alfred*);
- 892 – Alfred fights the Vikings again, but beats them with the army and his new navy;
- 937 – Alfred's great-grandson, King Edgar, becomes the first king of all England;
- Alfred introduces reading and writing to England;
- Sutton Hoo – the discovery of the ship in 1939. Children may want to construct a story about who the ship belonged to. The ending could be the burial of the thane with his ship.

■ Now think of an idea for the story. Here are some suggestions (the children will have more):

- use the same incident of the battle and siege at Edington, but with a girl as the main character;
- use the battle at Edington, but tell the story from a Viking boy's point of view;
- fourteen years later there is a battle against the Vikings, involving the navy – your character is involved. Wulfric is the captain.
- Saxon boy/girl going to the market at Chippenham to sell produce when the battle begins – how do they get home?

- When you have decided on ideas, plan the class story using OHT/poster 3. Explain to children that they are going to have a time plan to go with the story, so that they can use some of the time phrases they have found. Use the 'Time' word bank from Session 2.

- Plan the beginning of the story. Draw on children's knowledge about what goes into the beginning of a story (setting, character and problem). Decide whether there will be other characters in the story. Explain that you can add more characters as the story develops – the plan for the beginning should only contain details of the main characters.

- Move on to the ending. Ask children to consider some possible solutions to the problem. Do they want a happy ending with the problem solved, or a sad ending and an unresolved problem?

- Finally, plan the middle section. Ask children what happens to the characters in the story to lead them from the problem at the beginning to the planned ending. Remind the class that they will need a conflict/climax in the middle of the story. Try to limit the main events to four or five, as any more become unwieldy when writing a shared story.

- This is a sample plan from one of the suggested ideas:

BEGINNING	TIME

Characters: Ethelberga (Saxon girl)
                Edwin (Saxon boy) – brother and sister
                Fridrek (Viking boy)
                King Guthrum (Viking king)
Setting: Saxon village
             – just outside the Viking fort of Edington
Problem: Children go to market to sell apples.
             Saxons attack Vikings. Children are
             trapped inside fort and can't get home.
	
	day 1 (morning)
	day 1 (afternoon)

MIDDLE Children hide in house away from fighting. Found by Viking boy Fridrek – he hides them. Fridrek agrees to help them escape – plan a tunnel. Build tunnel under walls. *Climax* Start going through tunnel – caught by Viking soldiers. Taken to Viking King Guthrum.	 day 1 (night) day 2 (morning) 2 weeks day 14 (morning)
END Guthrum meets with Alfred to make peace. Children taken along to show Viking mercy. Siege ends, Vikings retreat. *Resolution* Children are taken home by Wulfric – trusted soldier of King Alfred.	 day 14 (afternoon) day 14 (evening)

Group follow-up activities   red/blue/yellow   **copymaster 1**

Children use copymaster 1 to plan their stories.

Guided group support

Red Provide the plan for the beginning of the story, using one of the ideas given in the shared session notes. Children can then concentrate on the end and the middle of the story. Limit the number of events in the middle of the story to three.

Blue Make children think carefully about the time plan for their story. Ensure sufficient time is given to each part of the story.

Yellow As with the blue group. Encourage children to plan five events in the middle section of their stories, leading up to a climax.

Alternative group activity   **red**

Children plan the story in pictures. They then write sentences next to each picture.

blue/yellow

Children use a large sheet of paper to plan the story on a story map. They identify the different sections of the story.

Plenary   Ask children what they have learnt about planning a story. Reinforce the concept of the beginning, middle and end, and stress that the middle section should include a conflict/climax. Ask some children to read out their story plans. The others listen critically to identify each section of the story.

---

⑥ Drafting the beginning of the story

Objectives   To learn to write an interesting story opening

To write a story beginning which orients the reader, sets the scene, introduces the characters and establishes a problem

Shared session   *You need: OHT/poster 6, OHT/poster 3 (saved from Session 5), OHT/poster 5 (saved from Session 4), 'Time' and 'Saxon' word bank posters, two large sheets of paper, two different colour marker pens.*

- ■ Tell children that you are going to learn how to write a good beginning for your story.

- ■ Refer to children's own experience of reading, and ask them what makes a good opening to a story. Tell children you are going to look at different methods which authors use to begin stories, to give them some ideas about how they might begin theirs.

- ■ Look at the story openings on OHT/poster 6. Read each one and ask the children how the author has opened the story – with **setting**, **dialogue**, **character** or **action** (*King Arthur* – character; *Beowulf* – dialogue; *The Last of the Vikings* – action). Remind children that *A Camp to Hide King Alfred* opens with a description of the setting.

- ■ Ask the children which way of opening the story they prefer, and why.

- ■ Refer back to the class story plan. (Children will also need to see the 'Time' and 'Saxon' word banks, as well as the class character profile.) Together, decide on the best way of opening your story.

■ Write the beginning of the story with the children, referring back constantly to the plan to ensure that all the information in the beginning of your plan has been included.

■ As you write, demonstrate **paragraphing**. The beginning of the story might be one paragraph, but if there is a change of time or place, you could discuss splitting the beginning of the story into more than one paragraph. Write alternate paragraphs in alternate colours.

■ As the story beginning develops, refer back to the personality of the main character, and decide whether to write some dialogue or action to reveal the character's personality to your readers.

■ This is a sample story beginning using the plan on page 32:

> "See you later," called Ethelberga as she and her younger brother Edwin leapt onto the cart. "Take care now, and mind you get at least five shillings for those apples at market," called their mother. The children waved goodbye, and fastened their woollen cloaks tightly around them. It was still early, and the sun's rays were only just beginning to warm the sky.
>
> An hour later the horse and cart rumbled into Melksham. Ethelberga hated coming to this market, as it was next to the Viking fort of Edington, and the Viking servants came to buy food there. Still, money was money, and her family needed it. Ethelberga and Edwin jumped down off the carts with their two baskets, and settled themselves in the marketplace. "Buy your apples, only one shilling for four!" shouted Edwin, trying to be heard above the noise of sheep, goats and chickens.
>
> After a lunch of bread and eggs, the children had only a few apples left to sell, and they were looking forward to going home. Suddenly there was an almighty noise and Viking warriors on horseback charged through the marketplace, flashing their swords and screaming loudly, "The Saxons are coming – all Vikings get into the fort!" Ethelberga and Edwin were afraid. They abandoned their apples, and tried to head out of the marketplace, but they were caught up in the frenzy of Vikings trying to get inside the fort. Before they knew it they had been swept along inside the fort itself. Ethelberga grabbed Edwin, and tried to get to the gate, but too late. It slammed shut. They were trapped!

Group follow-up activities   **red/blue/yellow**

Children use their plans to draft the beginning of their stories.

Guided group support

Red Help children to verbalise sentences before writing them down. Encourage them to use simple sentences.

Blue Focus on using children's story plans to ensure that they have included all necessary information. Beware of/point out assumptions that the reader knows what is happening, when insufficient detail has been given.

Yellow Develop children's use of paragraphing. Encourage them to split the beginning into more than one paragraph when there is a change of time or place.

Alternative group activity   **red**

Read the story beginning onto a tape which can later be played back and transcribed.

Plenary   Children read out their story beginnings. Set a listening target to identify which kind of opening has been used (e.g. dialogue, description). Is each beginning effective – do children want to know what happens next?

7 Drafting the middle and end of the story

Objectives   To write the middle and end of a story following a plan

To revise and extend the use of paragraphs

Shared session   *You need: story beginning draft, large sheets of paper, two different colour marker pens, OHT/poster 3 (from Session 6), OHT/poster 5 (saved from Session 4), 'Time' and 'Saxon' word bank posters.*

*1 See **Drafting** on page 6 for more detailed advice on conducting a whole-class drafting session.*

2 Children will write the main part of their stories in this session, so you may in fact want to spread this over two shared sessions – one to write the middle, and one to write the end. This will also give you extra guided writing sessions.

■ Look at the class plan. Revise what children know about paragraphs. Demonstrate that part of the way in which we organise a story is through paragraphs. Each of the main events in the plan could be a new paragraph, but as you write you may wish to insert more. Children are going to help you to decide when a new paragraph is needed.

■ Use the story beginning from the previous session, and continue with the shared writing, following the class plan. Write alternate paragraphs in alternate colours.

■ Invite ideas about how to pad out the 'bare bones' of the story which is contained in the plan. Refer back to the characters you created together. What would they do in certain situations? How do we show what they are like – through actions or speech/dialogue?

■ Use the 'Time' and 'Saxon' word banks and the character profile while you are writing. All these are supports which will help children with their own writing.

■ Ensure that the planned chronology is being followed.

■ Tell children that they are now going to continue to write their own stories. They will need to read back over the beginning of their story, and their plan <u>before</u> they start to write.

Group follow-up activities

You may wish to suggest that children write alternate paragraphs in pencil/pen. This physical changing of implements helps them to decide when to start a new paragraph.

red/blue/yellow

Children draft the middle and end of their stories.

Guided group support

Red Encourage children constantly to read their work aloud to a partner, so that they know what they have actually written, not what they <u>think</u> they have written, and that their writing makes sense.

Blue Focus on paragraphing. Using one of the children's story plans, decide with the group where a new paragraph may be needed. Demonstrate paragraph writing again if you think it is necessary.

Yellow Focus on characterisation. Help children add in more detail about characters. Try to move away from simple adjectives describing what the character looks like. Concentrate on showing personality through dialogue (include revision of speech marks, if necessary).

Plenary   Children read out their stories. Set the groups different 'listening targets':

- ◉ *Red* Think about which parts of the story are the beginning, middle and end.
- ◉ *Blue* Think about how you know the story has been set in Saxon/Viking times.
- ◉ *Yellow* Think about the characters, and the information that tells us what they are like.

After each story reading, start with positive feedback, and suggest one point for improvement. Invite positive comments from the other children.

8 Revising and editing the story

Objectives
To understand that writing can be improved by going back to it and working on it again

To consider the main points about writing historical stories, and to check whether these have been included in their writing

Shared session
You need: class story draft/child's story draft, 'Time' and 'Saxon' word banks, OHT/poster 5 (from Session 4), large sheets of paper.

*See **Revising and editing** on page 6 for more detailed advice.*

- Read through the class story, or one of the children's stories. Explain that you are going to look at the story again to make it as good as possible.

- Ask children whether the story is convincingly set in the past. Check that the story uses historically accurate language, and that there are no out-of-place modern words (**anachronisms**). Use the 'Saxon' word bank here, if necessary.

- Discuss the characters. Do we find out something about their personality, and whether we like them or not? If not, how could we change the writing to include more details about this? Use the character profile here.

- Now look at chronology. Is the time-scale realistic? Ask children if you need to alter it in any way, or perhaps insert some time phrases to clarify it. Use the 'Time' word bank here.

Group follow-up activities
red/blue/yellow   copymaster 4

Children practise using historically accurate language with the activity on copymaster 4.
They then work on revising and editing their own stories.

Guided group support

Red Help children look for anachronisms in their stories. Ensure events link together.

Blue As with the red group. Ask children to trace the chronology of their stories, inserting suitable time phrases where necessary.

Yellow Encourage children to look at the way the characters are portrayed in their stories, and to add in further detail to enhance characterisation if necessary.

Plenary
The children feed back on their revising and editing work, sharing what they have changed, and explaining how this has improved their stories.

9 Publishing the story

Objectives
To understand that there are different ways of publishing a story

To understand that illustrations must match the text

To produce a completed book

Shared session   *You need: a variety of historical story-books, large sheets of paper, different colour marker pens.*

1 See **Publishing** *on page 7 for more detailed notes on the issues involved in the final presentation of the text.*
2 *Here are some published story-books which you could look at in this session:* **The Saga of Leif Erikson** *by Roy Apps;* **King Arthur** *by Adrian Matthews;* **Norse Myths and Legends** *by Philip Ardagh;* **Beowulf** *by Kevin Crossley-Holland.*

■ Look at a variety of story-books – preferably historical ones. Look at the information on the front cover – title, author, illustrator. Note the size of fonts used. Look at the back of the book – blurb, price, etc.

■ Decide on illustrations to go with the story.

■ Decide how many pages you will need for the story. Mark which section of the story is going to be on each page, and make notes about illustrations. Use a large sheet of paper, marked off into the number of pages needed, with rough sketches and text layouts.

■ Refer back to the book covers you looked at earlier. Decide on the cover design, including large text to grab attention, author's name, etc. Ask children about the blurbs on the back of the published book covers. What are they for? Can they write one for this story?

Group follow-up activities   **red/blue/yellow**

Children work on publishing their stories.

Guided group support

Red Help children split their stories into reasonable page sections. Ensure that illustrations match text.

Blue As with the red group. Work with children to produce a striking front cover, and write a blurb.

Yellow Front cover and blurb as for the blue group. Encourage children to use adventurous text layouts and forms.

Plenary   Children read their completed books to the audience and enjoy them!

ADDITIONAL SESSIONS

Writing a diary entry for a historical character

Objectives   To write independently, linking own experience to situations in historical stories

To write from different points of view

To explore characterisation

Shared session (1)   *You need: OHTs/posters 1 and 2, a large sheet of paper.*

This session has been divided into two parts.

■ Tell children that they are going to write a personal diary entry for Wulfric or Eadgifu.

■ Ask children what they know about diaries. Discuss with them the different kinds of diaries (e.g. home reading diary, maths diary, appointment diary, personal diary). (N.B. Some children will keep their own personal diaries, and have a good understanding of the nature of personal diary writing; for others it is a difficult concept. The discussion about the type of writing they are going to produce is therefore vital.)

■ Ask children what they think should be written in a personal diary (e.g. hopes, fears, troubles, secrets). Stress that this is different from a simple diary of events which only tells us what happens. A personal diary contains a personal response to events.

- Ask children when personal diaries are written (e.g. daily, in times of trouble or happiness, when a major event occurs). Ask who the audience for a personal diary might be (e.g. the writer themselves, or perhaps a very trusted best friend).

- Establish that the purpose of personal diaries is to express personal thoughts and feelings about events.

- Explain that many people have written personal diaries in the past, and these have given us lots of historical information, as well as telling us how that person felt at the time. A famous example is *The Diary of Anne Frank*.

- Tell children that, now they have established the audience and purpose of a personal diary, they can decide what kind of writing they need to do. Establish that it will be informal and probably chronological.

- Now tell children that they are going to think about the events in *A Camp to Hide King Alfred* from Wulfric's point of view. Re-read the story (on OHT or poster).

- On a large sheet of paper, write two headings: 'Events' and 'Feelings'. Write short notes to show the main events, and ask the children how they think Wulfric would be feeling at these times in the story – for example:

Events	**Feelings**
– Wulfric in his hideaway	fed up, restless
– at the feast	excited, happy

- As you consider each event in the story, ask children to imagine how they would have felt. Relate Wulfric's experiences to the children's. For example, Wulfric's father says that he cannot fight with King Alfred. Have children ever been stopped from doing something that they really wanted to do? How did they feel? Does this help us to understand Wulfric's feelings?

- Ask a volunteer to hot-seat as Wulfric (or take on the role yourself). Other children then ask them questions about the events in the story and Wulfric's feelings about them. (This will provide a useful support for less able pupils when they come to write independently.)

Group follow-up activities (1)

1 red   Pupil's book page 12

Children choose words to describe Wulfric's feelings at different points in the story. They then complete sentences to explain these feelings.

Guided group support   Work together to choose different words to describe feelings. Use a thesaurus.

2 blue/yellow   Pupil's book page 13

Children write notes about Wulfric's or Eadgifu's feelings at different points in the story.

Guided group support

Blue As with the red group. Encourage children to think about how they would feel in the same situation – have they had experiences which caused similar feelings?

Yellow Encourage the children to consider events from Eadgifu's perspective. Ask them to consider the same events from other characters' points of view (e.g. Wulfric's mother and father, Wynflaed, King Alfred).

Plenary (1)

Ask two volunteers to sit in the hot-seat as Wulfric and Eadgifu. The rest of the class asks them questions about their thoughts and feelings at key points in the story. Emphasise the different points of view expressed by the two characters.

Shared session (2) *You need: 'Events' and 'Feelings' sheet (from previous shared session).*

■ Recap on what children learnt about personal diaries in the previous shared session.

■ Establish the audience for the children's personal diary entries for Wulfric or Eadgifu (e.g. other children in the class; a parallel class). Explain that, as this is a personal diary of a fictional character, we may write it for other people to read. This is different from a personal diary which we might write, which would probably be for our own private reading (or for a trusted friend).

■ Establish the time-scale of the diary. Refer back to the work done on chronology in Session 2 of the main focus. Depending on the ability of your class, you can either split the diary entry into sections and insert dates, writing an entry after each key point in the story (more able), or write only one entry, written retrospectively after all the events (less able).

■ Ask children how they think the piece should start. Do they want simply to begin writing their thoughts, or do they want to start with 'Dear Diary'? They may wish to give their diary a name, as Anne Frank did, and write to it in the style of a letter to a best friend.

■ Write the beginning of the diary entry together, stressing the style of the piece. Emphasise to children that they are writing as the character: the writing should be in the first person.

■ Refer back as necessary to the notes about feelings which you made in the previous shared session.

Group follow-up activities (2) red

Children write the diary entry for Wulfric, using the work they did in shared session 1, and the shared work as support.

Guided group support Help children write the diary entry in the first person. It may help to get them to write one entry only, covering all the events in the story.

blue/yellow

Children write the diary entry for Wulfric or Eadgifu, using the work in shared session 1 as support.

Guided group support

Blue As with the red group. Encourage children to include as much detail as possible about their character's feelings.

Yellow Ask children to split the diary into small sections. Help them to use future and past tense simultaneously in these sections. For example, after Wulfric takes the King to his hiding place he may write: *It has been a very tiring, but exciting day. I hope that I will be strong and brave enough to protect the King.*

Plenary (2) Ask children what they have learnt from writing the diary entry of a historical character. Discuss any difficulties which occurred during the writing. Ask children to share some of their work to illustrate different points of view.

Writing a playscript from the story

Objectives   To revise the organisation of playscripts

To write a playscript with a historical setting

To develop characterisation through dialogue

Shared session   *You need: a large sheet of paper for class poster, OHT/poster 1 (and paper to mask text).*

■   Explain that you are going to work together to write the beginning of *A Camp to Hide King Alfred* as a play.

■   Revise the purpose of a play (to entertain and, sometimes, to inform).

■   Ask children what they know about how a playscript is organised (revision from Year 3 Term 1) and write up their ideas on a poster. This will be a useful reference point for children when they write independently.

■   Establish that:

  ○   the story is told in dialogue;

  ○   there are no speech marks;

  ○   there may be a narrator;

  ○   there are stage directions, telling us how the stage should appear, and how the actors should say their lines and move.

■   Return to OHT/poster 1, masking the text from *Wulfric's father Aelfwin was master of the hall*. Ask children to identify the characters in the text (Wulfric, Eadgifu, father (Aelfwin), mother, youth (Wynflaed), guests at the feast).

■   Establish that a list of characters in a play is called the **cast**. Write the cast list for this play on the poster. Ask children if they can think of another character they might want to tell parts of the story to the audience (i.e. the narrator). Add this to the cast list, but stress that it is optional.

■   Ask children where the action takes place at the beginning of the story (in the hideaway; in the hall at the feast). Draw boxes around these two sections and tell children that a change of setting in a story often means a change of **scene** in a play. Write 'Scene 1' and 'Scene 2' on the appropriate sections of the text.

■   Look at the first section. Ask children how Wulfric is feeling at the beginning of the story. Underline the key words and phrases which tell you this (e.g. *get away from his younger sister*; *thought longingly of becoming a soldier*).

■   Ask how you are going to show Wulfric's character in the first scene – in the narrative he does not speak. Discuss with children what he might say to reveal how he is feeling, and emphasise that characterisation can be shown through dialogue.

■   Write scene 1 and scene 2 with the class, discussing the layout of the character's names and dialogue and the use of stage directions as you proceed.

■   Scene 1 may look something like this:

Scene 1: An island in the Somerset marshes

(It is sunset. Wulfric is alone in his hideaway among the reeds and rushes.)

Wulfric: At last, a bit of peace and quiet. I wonder if everyone's sister is as annoying as mine? I wish I could join Alfred's army. I'd be good, I know I would. I'm sick of hanging around at home and being bossed about. I'm old enough to be a soldier now – it's not fair! Oh no! It's nearly dark, and I'm going to be late for the feast. My dad's going to be furious.

(Wulfric gets in his boat and rows furiously back to the village.)

Group follow-up activities

It will be easier for the average and less able children to work from the model text, as there is a strong story-line, and support has been given in the shared session. The more able children should work from their own stories.

1 red   Pupil's book page 14

Children use the play outline in the pupil's book to write scenes 1 and 2. They may need to re-read the text from OHT/poster 1 to support them. They work in pairs to speak the dialogue first, then write it. Finally, they act out the two scenes.

Guided group support   Help children set the playscript out correctly.

2 blue   Pupil's book page 15   copymaster 5

Children read the next part of *A Camp to Hide King Alfred*. They plan the play on copymaster 5, which provides support as it is divided into the four scenes given in the text (in the bower, the journey to the camp, in the village, by the marsh). They then write the scenes as playscripts, and finally act them out.

Guided group support   Help children to set the playscript out correctly, making decisions about scenes and characters. Encourage them to use dialogue to show characterisation.

3 yellow   Pupil's book page 16   copymaster 5

Children re-read their own stories with historical settings. They plan the play on copymaster 5, then write it. If children need more scenes in their play, they can use the back of the copymaster and continue to plan in the same format. They then perform their plays.

Guided group support   Help children use dialogue and stage directions to show action and characterisation.

Plenary   Ask children what they have learnt about writing a playscript, particularly about the layout of playscripts, and how to show characters' feelings through what they say. Ask children to act out their scenes or plays. The rest of the class listens critically to the dialogue to assess the characterisation.

Using imagination or experience to write a poem

Objectives   To investigate powerful verbs

To write, expand and contract descriptive phrases

To write a poem about an animal

Shared session (1)   *You need: OHT/poster 7, five pieces of card (see below), a large sheet of paper, pictures/photographs of animals (optional).*

■   Explain that you are going to write poems about animals. These can either be about pets the children own or would like to own, or about an imagined animal. Establish an audience for your poems.

1 If possible, children should read poems about animals, written in different forms, before starting work on this additional session. It would also be useful if children have already done work on 'powerful' verbs.

2 You may wish to link work done here to a science topic, such as 'Moving and growing', or 'Habitats'.

3 This session has been divided into two parts.

■ Read the poem 'Badgers', by Richard Edwards, on OHT/poster 7. Ask children for their responses to the poem. Which words and phrases do they like? What can they tell about badgers from the poem?

■ Now discuss the form of the poem with the children. Ask them:

 ◉ How many lines are there in each verse? (Three.)

 ◉ What is the same about the beginning of most lines? (The word *Badgers*.)

 ◉ What is the rhyme scheme for each verse? (The final word of each line rhymes.)

■ Tell children that they are going to use this structure, or part of it, when they write their own poems.

■ Ask children to identify the verbs in the poem and underline them. Discuss the effect of the verbs – for example, why does the poet choose *creeping* instead of *walking* in the first line? (Because it tells us clearly how the badger is moving. This helps to create a visual image of the badger in our heads.)

■ Emphasise that the choice of words in a poem is very important. Children are going to be 'painting a picture' of an animal using words, so they need to take care when choosing verbs to describe the actions of their animal.

■ Look at the last line of each verse. Ask children what they notice about it (it is shorter than the others). Tell children that you are going to experiment with one of these lines, to see if you can make it longer or shorter.

■ Write the words *Badgers*, *go*, *nosing* and *around* on four pieces of card, and ask children to hold them. Ask the class if there is any way that the line could be made shorter, but still keep its meaning. Experiment with taking out *go* and *around*. Similarly, ask children for words to insert to make the line longer (e.g. *busily*). Write suggestions on pieces of card and ask more volunteers to hold them up with the others. Ask children which version of this line is the most effective and why.

■ Decide on an animal to write the class poem about (if possible, have some pictures to hand). Tell children that, before you write the poem, you need to brainstorm words and phrases to describe the animal. Use a large sheet of paper to write up children's suggestions. Write the verbs in a separate list.

■ Tell children that they are now going to brainstorm words and phrases about their animal in preparation for writing their poems.

Group follow-up activities (1) red/blue/yellow   Pupil's book page 17

This activity is ideal for group and pair work. The children could work on a large piece of paper with marker pens and discuss their ideas. It also works well with mixed ability groups

Children look at the animals in the pupil's book or choose one of their own (either a pet they own/would like to own, or another animal they can imagine). They complete a chart with words and phrases to describe their animal.

Guided group support

Red Help children write descriptive phrases for each section of the chart.

Blue Encourage children to use powerful verbs, and to experiment with descriptive phrases by expanding and contracting for effect.

Yellow As with the blue group. Look at the effect of substituting different powerful verbs.

Plenary (1) Display children's work. Use it to discuss the words and phrases they have written. Look specifically at the verbs they have chosen and discuss the reasons for their choices.

Shared session (2) *You need: animal word list (from shared session 1), OHT/poster 7, large sheets of paper.*

■ Tell children you are now ready to write the class poem about your chosen animal. Recap on the list of words and phrases which you brainstormed in the previous session.

■ Look again at the structure of the poem 'Badgers'. Discuss which parts of the structure you want to use. You may want to use the three line verses, the animal's name at the beginning of the line and the rhyme scheme. Alternatively, you may want to change the rhyme scheme and verse structure, while keeping the animal's name at the beginning of each line. The writing will be just as effective either way.

■ Write the poem together. Re-read the poem aloud as you write, crossing out and redrafting continuously if better words/phrases are suggested.

■ Read the completed class poem with the children.

Group follow-up activities (2) **red/blue/yellow**

Children use their work from the previous session to write their poem.

Guided group support

Red Write the animal's name at the beginning of each line to reinforce the structure. This will prevent the poem from becoming a narrative.

Blue Help children to use descriptive phrases, and to redraft constantly, improving their work as they write.

Yellow As with the blue group.

Plenary (2) Ask children what they have learnt about how to write descriptive poems. Listen to some of the children's poems and write down any words or phrases which children find interesting or unusual. Keep this word bank as a class resource.

Homework suggestions

● Choose a story-book you have at home, or use your home reading book. Write a plan of the story. Identify the conflict/climax in the middle section. (**After Session 1**)

● Think of a story you know well – for example, 'Cinderella'. Write a plan of the story. Identify the conflict/climax in the middle section. (**After Session 1**)

● Choose a story-book you have at home, or use your home reading book. Collect time phrases for the class chart. (**After Session 2**)

● Use copymaster 2 and make up some more time phrases of your own. (**After Session 2**)

● Think of where you might set your historical story. Draw and label this setting, using appropriate vocabulary. (**After Session 3**)

● Create another character for your story. Write a character profile for him/her on copymaster 3. (**After Session 4**)

● Take home a copy of your story. Read through it to make sure that the spelling is correct and the vocabulary is historically accurate. (**After Session 8**)

● Look at some historical story-books which have interesting ways of presenting text and illustrations. Bring them to school to look at in class. (**After Session 8**)

● Draw some plans for the layout of the pages in your story. Think about the title page and where illustrations could go. (**After Session 8**)

UNIT 1 How to write a historical story

Colour the right number of stars to show how well you did the following things:

0 stars = I didn't do it.   3 stars = I did it well.
1 star = I gave it a try.   4 stars = I did an excellent job!
2 stars = I did it quite well.

I planned my story clearly.	☆	☆	☆	☆
I set my story in a historical period.	☆	☆	☆	☆
I wrote an interesting story opening.	☆	☆	☆	☆
The middle of my story built up to a climax.	☆	☆	☆	☆
I wrote in paragraphs.	☆	☆	☆	☆
I showed my characters' personalities.	☆	☆	☆	☆
I used time phrases.	☆	☆	☆	☆

Something I am especially pleased with

Something my audience liked in my writing

Something I'd like to do better next time

Term one non-fiction focus:
2 How to write a newspaper-style recount

What most children will already know:

Recounts are non-fiction texts that retell true events.
The structure of recounts generally includes:

- an orientation;
- events in chronological order;
- a reorientation.

Recounts are written in the past tense.
Recounts usually refer to specific participants.

What children will learn in this unit:

Newspaper articles featuring 'news' are often impersonal recounts.

Newspaper recounts are written in a 'high impact' journalistic style.

Newspaper recounts often feature a present tense reorientation.

Newspaper recounts also include headlines and captions.

Headlines and captions are often written using shortened sentences.

1 Looking at the structure of newspaper-style recounts

Objectives To identify the structural features and layout of a recount article

To generate a framework for children's own writing

Shared session *You need: OHT/poster 8.*

In preparation for this unit, children should have read some newspaper articles. If possible, bring in a few articles, preferably from a variety of newspapers, to show different writing styles.

- Explain to children that they are going to write a newspaper article. First of all you are going to analyse an article together to give children a model for their writing.

- Display OHT/poster 8 ('Cat-napping kitten gets carried away'), masking the text so that only the photo and headline can be seen. Ask children what the article might be about.

- Now read the text on OHT/poster 8 and ask a few questions to check understanding – for example:
  - Who is Megan? Where did she come from?
  - How far did she travel?
  - Did the car owner know she was there?

- Ask children whether they think this article is about a very important event for a lot of people (no). So why do they think it was published in a newspaper? (People will be interested; it's fun.) Explain that this kind of report is called a **human interest** story.

- Ask children to identify the **headline**. Draw a box around it on the OHT and label it 'headline'. Point out that the font is larger and bolder than the rest of the text. Ask what the purpose of a headline is (to catch the reader's eye; to make them want to read more; to give some idea of what the article is about).

- Ask children to identify the **photo**. Box and label it. Ask children why they think it is there (for visual appeal and to give information). What can we learn from this photo? (Who the article is about and what she looks like.)

- Ask children to identify the **caption**. Box and label it. What is its purpose? (It acts as a label for the picture, identifies Megan and gives some information.)

- Ask children if they think Megan really has nine lives, and explain the expression if necessary. Point out that a 'jokey' style is common in captions for this type of article.

- Ask children to recap on the information given in a recount orientation: it establishes *who, what, where* and *when*. Ask them to find out which of these questions are answered in the first paragraph. Underline the information which answers each question (there are answers for *who, what* and *where*).

- Box and label this part of the text as the **orientation**. Ask what purpose it has. (It sets the scene and summarises the main points of the article.)

- Box and label the **main body** of the text and ask children to think about what this section tells us as you re-read it. (It tells the whole story with interesting details and some explanation.) It usually answers the questions *how* and *why*.

- Box and label the **reorientation**. Re-read it and ask children what they think its purpose is (to conclude the retelling of events and bring them up-to-date).

- Point out that this kind of article often includes some comment by the people involved in the story. Ask children to identify the quote in direct speech (*"Megan is feeling much better now..."*).

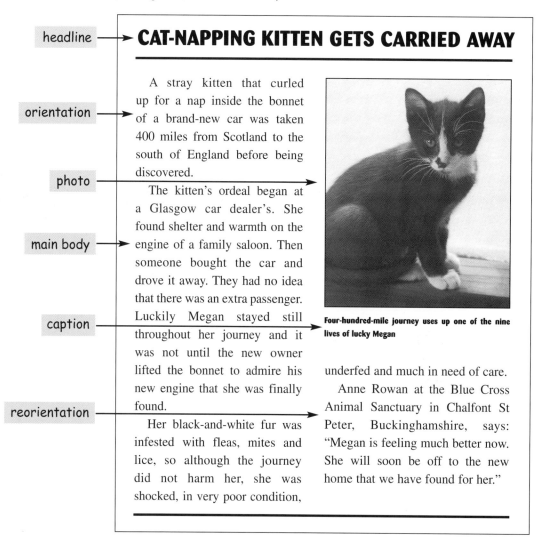

headline →

CAT-NAPPING KITTEN GETS CARRIED AWAY

orientation →

A stray kitten that curled up for a nap inside the bonnet of a brand-new car was taken 400 miles from Scotland to the south of England before being discovered.

photo →

main body →

The kitten's ordeal began at a Glasgow car dealer's. She found shelter and warmth on the engine of a family saloon. Then someone bought the car and drove it away. They had no idea that there was an extra passenger.

caption →

Luckily Megan stayed still throughout her journey and it was not until the new owner lifted the bonnet to admire his new engine that she was finally found.

reorientation →

Her black-and-white fur was infested with fleas, mites and lice, so although the journey did not harm her, she was shocked, in very poor condition,

Four-hundred-mile journey uses up one of the nine lives of lucky Megan

underfed and much in need of care.

Anne Rowan at the Blue Cross Animal Sanctuary in Chalfont St Peter, Buckinghamshire, says: "Megan is feeling much better now. She will soon be off to the new home that we have found for her."

Group follow-up activities   1 red   Pupil's book page 18   copymasters 6 and 7

Children cut up the article on copymaster 6 and stick each section into the correct place on copymaster 7.

Guided group support Consolidate children's understanding of the recount framework, especially the way in which the orientation summarises the points given in the main body of the text.

2 blue/yellow   Pupil's book page 18

Children reconstruct the jumbled text. They write down the correct sequence, then label each part of the text *orientation*, *main body* or *reorientation*.

Guided group support Look at the relationship between the three main parts of the text, comparing and contrasting the orientation with the reorientation. Discuss how a story is concluded by bringing it up-to-date.

3 yellow   Pupil's book page 19

As activity 2, using a more challenging text.

Guided group support As for activity 2, but extend consideration of the reorientation to include the idea of projecting events into the future (e.g. the closing line of the article contains a prediction about Keiko's future).

Plenary Start compiling a 'Journalistic recount' poster. Recap the various sections of a newspaper-style recount and elicit the features of each. Include headline, photo, caption, orientation, main body and reorientation.

Section	Features and purpose
headline	• large, bold print, eye-catching • create interest, give information
caption	• labels the picture • sometimes in a jokey style
etc.	

② Identifying key features – headlines, photos and captions

Objectives   To identify specific examples of journalistic language and consider their impact

To investigate the shortened language conventions of headlines and captions

Shared session   *You need: OHT/poster 9.*

■ Display and read the headlines on OHT/poster 9, masking the photo at the bottom.

■ Ask children whether headlines are full sentences. (No, they usually use a short form.) Ask them why. (Content is presented dramatically to convey the key point and to 'hook' the reader.)

■ Together, expand a sample headline to a full sentence – for example, *There has been an earthquake in Japan.*

■ Discuss briefly what each article might be about. Ask children which of the headlines works best at arousing their interest, and why.

■ Focus on 'Fangs a lot!' and ask what *fangs* sounds like. Ask children why they think the journalist chose this headline. (It helps get across two ideas at once.) Explain that headlines often use word-play such as puns, alliteration and rhyme to attract attention and to introduce content as briefly as possible. Draw attention to the use of alliteration in 'Shell-shocked' and 'Battle of the burger'.

- Uncover the photo. Let children match it with the appropriate headline ('Shell-shocked') and ask what the picture tells us. Discuss the way a photo can arouse interest and convey information that, if conveyed through words alone, might make the article very long and complicated. Point out that the photo also makes clear the word-play in the headline.

- Ask what information the photo caption gives the reader about the story. (It identifies participants by name and briefly explains the situation.)

- Focus on the style of the caption. (It is like a label – key words, bare minimum to explain the photo; it 'gets straight to the point'.)

Group follow-up activities

1 red   Pupil's book page 20

Children write captions and headlines for two photos.

Guided group support Encourage children to give names to the people and places in the photos. Help them to write as briefly as possible about what the picture shows. Focus on language structures for the headlines, helping children to delete appropriate words to make them short and snappy

2 blue/yellow   Pupil's book page 21

Children read the orientation section of four newspaper articles and make up headlines to go with them.

Guided group support Discuss when readers might expect serious headlines and captions, and when they might enjoy some fun. Use a thesaurus and try out a range of word-play ideas to create a bank of entertaining ideas for one topic.

3 yellow   Pupil's book page 22

Children identify 'headlines' based on nursery rhymes or traditional tales. They then try writing some of their own.

Guided group support As for activity 2, but move on to brainstorm some serious and dramatic headlines. Experiment with one-word headlines.

Plenary Ask children to recap on the features of headlines, photos and captions and add this information to your poster. All groups feed back on some of their headlines and the rest of the class evaluates the writing.

(3) Identifying key language features – orientation, main body and reorientation

Objectives To analyse language used in each part of a newspaper-style recount

To show chronological order through chronological connectives

To learn how to round off an article

Shared session *You need: OHT/poster 8 (saved from Session 1).*

- Tell children that you are going to look in more detail at the language of each section of the report, and think about how it all fits together.

- Re-read with the children the headline and orientation section of the text on OHT/poster 8. Focus on the link between the headline and the orientation section by asking children to explain what the headline means.

- Ask children to recap on the purpose of the orientation. (*Who, what, where* and *when* – it's a short summary of all the key information that is examined in more detail in the rest of the article.)

- Point out that since the orientation gives readers an overview of the story and helps them decide whether they want to read more, it is important to keep it brief (often one extended sentence) and 'high impact'. Ask children to identify the points in this orientation that help to get the reader interested (e.g. *stray kitten, a brand-new car, 400 miles*).

- Focus on the main text and recap what this section tells us (*how* and *why*). Ask what additional details are added in this section and discuss the interest they create for the reader.

- Recap that events in recounts are presented in **chronological order** and ask children to identify and underline the words in the main text that help the reader understand the sequence of events (*first, then, finally*).

- Ask children if they know any more of these time linking words (*next, afterwards*, etc)

- Ask children to identify and underline some of the verbs in the main text. What tense are they in, and why? (e.g. *began, found, bought*. The verbs are in the past tense because they retell events from the past.)

- Focus on the reorientation and ask children to recap on its purpose. (It is a conclusion that brings the retelling up-to-date.)

- Ask children to find and underline the present tense verbs in this section (*says, is feeling*) Why are they used here? (The focus has switched from what happened in the past to how things are now, after the reported events.)

- Note too that many reorientations move into the future by referring to what participants plan to do, or what they hope will happen (*She will soon be off...*).

Group follow-up activities

1 red   Pupil's book page 23

Children write an orientation section for one of the photos for which they wrote a headline and caption in the previous session.

Guided group support Focus on summary skills. Ensure children include *who, what, where* and *when*.

2 blue/yellow   Pupil's book page 23

Children write orientations for two headlines – one serious and one humorous.

Guided group support

Blue Discuss the differences in style between the headlines and help children make sure they reflect this in their orientation sections.

3 yellow   Pupil's book page 24

Children now write an orientation section for a 'catchy' headline which gives little or no information about the story.

Plenary Recap on the key features of a good orientation and add this information to your poster. Ask each group to present one of their orientations to be evaluated by the rest of the class according to these criteria.

4 Planning the recount

Objective To introduce a question-word content planner for a recount text

Shared session *You need: OHT/poster 10, a large sheet of paper or blank OHT.*

It will be very helpful for the children in the planning and writing of their articles if you are able to take or obtain some photos of events of interest to the school/community that they may wish to write about.

- Explain to children that you are first going to write a newspaper article together. Then they will be writing an article of their own. Tell them how and where their articles will be published. (Photocopied and displayed, copies made for all the students, etc.) Recap on the audience – who are they writing for? (e.g. another class, the whole school, parents.)

- Tell children that, as an example, you are going to look at a photo of an event at another school. Then they are going to think about a real event at their own school. Display the photo on OHT/poster 10, masking the chart below it.

- Ask children if they can remember the key questions that need answering in the orientation section (*who, what, where, when*). Reveal the chart on OHT/poster 10.

- Ask children to help you fill in the chart for the event shown in the photo, getting as much information as they can from the photo and headline and making up any further details. The completed chart might look like this:

Who?	What?	Where?	When?	Why?	How?
90 pupils at Milton Road Junior School	Held a sponsored skip	In the school playground	After school last Friday	To raise money for a new computer suite	Each child skipped for 15 minutes, then had a rest

- Next, ask children to think of a recent activity at your own school or in the local community – for example, a school trip, a school play or concert, a fund-raising event, a football match.

- Fill in the chart for the new (real) report together. (Either write on OHT/poster 10 in a different colour beneath your existing notes or work on a clean copy on a large sheet of paper or blank OHT.) Remind children to think about the audience they have agreed to write for – are there any specific details that they might be particularly interested in?

- Explain that the 'Why' and 'How' columns are of particular importance to the length and 'depth' of a newspaper recount – they give the interesting and informative facts of the story.

Group follow-up activities **1 red/blue/yellow Pupil's book page 25**

All groups start to plan their own newspaper article, using the grid in the pupil's book as a model.

Guided group support

Red Help children to think of an event that they want to write about. Encourage them to talk through their ideas with you and with each other. Remind children to make notes using just a few key words.

Blue/Yellow As for the red group but ensure that a good level of detail is being added to the planning grid.

Plenary Ask one group to demonstrate how they have used the planning grid. Ask them to talk about how easy or difficult it was and why.

5 Transferring planning information to a recount framework

Objective To plan the article using the recount framework

Shared session *You need: an enlarged version of copymaster 7, completed class planning framework (from Session 4).*

- Display the enlarged version of copymaster 7. Tell children that you are going to leave the headline, photo and caption until later. Explain that it is sensible to start with the orientation because its content may influence the headline.

- Recap that the orientation answers the questions *who, what, where* and *when*. Refer back to the planning grid from the previous session and transfer the relevant information onto the new frame (excluding the *why* and *how* notes).

- Now plan the main body of the text. Recap that this section will contain key events in chronological order, and will add as many details as possible to hold the reader's interest. It will refer to information about *who, what, where* and *when* already incorporated in the orientation, but it will rely mainly on details from the 'Why' and 'How' columns. Refer to your planning frame frequently as you work.

- Encourage children to include as much detail as possible to elaborate on the basic summary in the orientation, asking questions like:
  - Why did the event take place?
  - Who organised it?
  - Who else was involved?
  - How did participants arrive at or leave the event?
  - What results might there be?
  - What other details might readers want to know?

- Finally, move on to the reorientation. Recap on the main purpose of this section and ask how the story can be 'brought up to date' or predict future events (e.g. what the money raised will be used for, how children look forward to using the new equipment, what children have learnt from the school trip).

Group follow-up activities **red/blue/yellow**   **copymaster 7**

Children continue to plan their recounts. All groups fill in copymaster 7, transferring the relevant information from their planning frameworks as demonstrated in the shared session.

Guided group support

Red Help children to make sure they have organised the points in the main body of the text in chronological order.

Blue/Yellow Work to ensure that a good level of detail is noted down for the main recount section and for the reorientation.

Plenary Groups feed back on the decisions they have made and explain why they made them.

6 Drafting the recount

Objectives

To use 'high impact' language

To use photos and interview quotes to add impact

To adopt an appropriate level of formality

To adopt a particular tone in writing – chatty, serious, entertaining, etc.

Shared session

You need: the enlarged version of copymaster 7, filled in from the previous session, a large sheet of paper for drafting, marked up with the planning framework (or another enlarged version of copymaster 7).

■ Recap with children on the audience for the text they are working on and its purpose (to inform? to entertain?). Discuss what kind of language their audience will expect (e.g. humorous and sensational, or respectable and sensible). If children looked at different styles of newspapers when working on reading objectives for this term, you may like to refer to these.

■ If you are using a photo, paste it onto the 'photo' space on the planning framework (i.e. the marked-up one on the large sheet of paper, or the enlarged version of copymaster 7). If not, discuss what kind of photo would be appropriate, and note this in the space.

■ Briefly explain and demonstrate the way in which the *who, what, where, when* notes on the planning framework can be expanded to provide a summary sentence for the orientation. Show how you can manipulate the order in which the answers to *who, what, where* and *when* appear – for example:

> 90 pupils at Milton Road Junior School → held a sponsored skip → in the school playground → after school last Friday.

> After school last Friday → a sponsored skip was held → in the school playground → by 90 pupils at Milton Road Junior School.

■ Together, experiment with several versions of the summary sentence to see which works best. You may find it helpful actually to cut the planning grid that you produced in Session 4 into separate columns which can be moved around to illustrate this point.

■ Elicit ideas for a photo caption and write the agreed version below the photo.

■ Discuss what information should go in the headline. Bearing in mind what you have agreed about audience and style, recap on the important features of a headline and elicit some ideas. Can any of these be embellished and developed with word-play? Write the most appropriate headline on the planning framework.

■ Write up the main body of the text, referring constantly to the planning framework in order to model the process of developing text from planning notes. Ask how you can help the reader understand the sequence of events and add in some chronological connectives (*first, next,* etc.).

■ Focus on the reorientation. Use the notes from the previous session and ask children to expand them into one or two sentences. If necessary remind them about the verb tense shift into the present and future – for example, *The head teacher is delighted with the money that the children raised. All the children are looking forward to using their new computer suite early next term.*

- The reorientation might include a suitable quote from someone who took part in the event – for example, *The head teacher said, "Children enjoyed the skipping and I know that they will love using the new computers."* Point out that, when children write their own reports, they might choose to interview someone who was there to get this kind of quote.

- Work with children to make sure that the final sentence is both effective and memorable.

Group follow-up activities   Children work on drafting their recounts. Provide them with any photos you have managed to obtain.

Guided group support

Red Compose a group 'who/what/where/when' planning grid and cut it into strips. Shuffle the pieces into a different order each time, and make up an appropriate summary sentence for the orientation. Help children make good use of connectives in drafting the main body of the text.

Blue Encourage children to check that they have organised the events of the main text in chronological order, using appropriate connectives. Encourage them to incorporate all the details from their planning framework in a coherent way.

Yellow Consider style and language carefully, trying to ensure consistency of tone. Work to ensure the reorientation rounds off the piece as effectively as possible.

Plenary   Groups/individuals present their headlines and orientation sections for evaluation by the rest of the class. Ask for feedback on one way in which the writer has succeeded in appealing to the reader and ask for one suggestion for improvement.

⑦ Revising and editing the recount

Objectives   To revise written work, according to stated audience and purpose

To maximise the effects of journalistic style and 'high impact' language

Shared session   *You need: class draft from previous session.*

See **Revising and editing** on page 6 for more detailed advice.

- Tell children that they have done extremely good work so far, but remind them that all real journalists have to 'tweak' their writing for maximum impact on the intended audience. Tell children their job is now to read and listen as newspaper readers and try to assess the strengths and weaknesses of their work so far.

- Display the class draft and recap briefly on all the characteristics of journalistic text which you have identified and tried to reproduce.

- Ask children to think about how the article can be improved as you read the first draft of the text. Focus on the following points:
  - **Headline:** is it snappy, attention-grabbing, informative?
  - **Caption:** is it interesting?
  - **Orientation:** does it give enough information? Is it clear, concise and informative? Does it entice the reader to go on?
  - **Main body:** are the events related in a logical (chronological) order? Have you included enough details to keep the audience adequately informed?
  - **General:** is the language appropriate for the target audience? Is it (if appropriate) entertaining, intriguing, striking, emphatic? Is the tone and style of the piece just what you wanted?

■ Work with a different colour marker pen so children can track changes as they are made. Keep reading the 'before' and 'after' versions of each textual element as you change it so that children can see, hear and really feel the improvements.

■ Encourage children to say what they like and dislike about how the text is changing. Make as many changes as necessary for a clear majority to feel satisfied with the finished product.

Group follow-up activities All groups work on their own texts, 'echoing' the improvement process modelled in the shared session.

Guided group support

Red Help children to identify just one or two weaknesses in their work. Practical support in improving the text is usually the most convincing way of proving the value of textual revision, so give children some suggestions to try out.

Blue Focus on a few of the key words, especially any intended to evoke an emotional response. Take a few sample sentences and re-work them for maximum impact.

Yellow As with the blue group but work to develop control and promote consistency of tone and style throughout the piece.

Plenary Ask volunteers to contribute examples of changes they have made to their texts, explaining what they feel was the original textual weakness. Other children contribute reactions to the 'before' and 'after' versions, commenting as target readers on whether these improvements have been effective.

⑧ Publishing the recount

Objectives To decide how to present journalistic text and a picture

To experiment with font styles, sizes and highlighting effects for visual appeal

To edit text on screen to fit a given space

Shared session Using ICT

*1 See **Publishing** on page 7 for more detailed notes on the issues involved in the final presentation of the text.*

2 If using ICT, you may wish to type in the class text and scan in any photos in advance of this session.

■ Ideally, work on one monitor for this shared session (depending on your school's ICT arrangements).

■ Your session is likely to include the following:

  o making the whole text fit a given page size, as required for publication;

  o showing the children how to change fonts;

  o experimenting with *Wordart* (or similar) to enhance the appearance of headlines.

■ You should conduct ongoing comment and discussion about the effectiveness of each change.

■ Use spelling (and grammar) checkers to make a final edit.

■ Print out the agreed version of the shared text. If possible, arrange multiple photocopying so each child has a copy.

Publication without ICT

■ Ask children to produce work on A4 paper.

■ Trim off any excess paper and assemble several children's articles onto A3 paper. Photocopy these as two-sided sheets. Fold into a simple A4 'newspaper' and use a long-armed stapler to fix the pages together at the 'spine'.

■ Print and staple enough copies for each child to have one, making some extra copies for the school library or for display.

Group follow-up activities   All groups work on the presentation of their own newspaper/ magazine articles.

Guided group support

Red Children in this group sometimes excel at presentational activities, and this may be particularly the case when supported by ICT. This session provides an excellent opportunity for teachers to channel enthusiasm and bolster feelings of success.

Blue Help children to assess their articles (and presentation) from their readers' point of view. Direct their attention to specific issues such as how easy a font is to read, whether the headline looks disproportionately large, etc.

Yellow Children could be supported in analysing and recreating a particular presentational style – perhaps that of the local paper, or a well-known daily.

Plenary   Display the articles so that children can read and comment on each other's work.

ADDITIONAL SESSIONS

Writing a report

Objectives   To recap on the main features of non-chronological reports

To use information gained from reading to write a report, making decisions on what to include and what to omit

To include organisational devices such as headings and numbered lists

To ensure clarity and conciseness

Shared session (1)   *You need: OHTs/posters 8 and 11.*

*1 This session provides revision of **How to write a non-chronological report** (Year 3, Term 2).*
2 This session has been divided into two parts.

■ See if children can remember what happened to Megan the kitten at the end of her ordeal (see OHT/poster 8 – she was cared for by the Blue Cross Animal Sanctuary).

■ Tell children that animal care organisations like the Blue Cross have to write notes about each animal that is brought in to them. Together, you are going to write a report about Megan. Its purpose is to help the Blue Cross decide what to do with her. Children should think about how this writing will differ in style from the newspaper report.

■ Display the standard framework for a non-chronological report on OHT/poster 11. Then ask the children to recap what should go in each section:

Opening statement: a general statement which summarises what the report is about.

Information section:	facts about the subject.
	Information is divided into smaller sections, each with a different focus.
	These sections are often given headings.
	Information is not arranged in chronological order (but it needs to be in a sensible order).
Closing section:	a conclusion which 'rounds off' the report, often finishing with some points of particular interest.

- On OHT/poster 11, start to plan out with children what will go in the report about Megan. Decide what should go in the opening statement (who Megan is, and the purpose of the report, i.e. to decide what to do with her).

- Decide on three main topics to include in the information section, based on what you know from the newspaper article and bearing in mind the purpose of the report (e.g. 'More about Megan', 'What is wrong with her', 'What she needs').

- The closing section could contain a recommendation about what to do with Megan.

Group follow-up activities (1)

1 red/blue   Pupil's book page 26

Children read a report text and decide on the most appropriate heading for each section. They then decide on a heading for one section which does not have one.

Guided group support

Red/Blue Ask children to identify the purpose of the report. Help them to identify the relationship between the final recommendation and the positive information in the other paragraphs.

Discuss how the headings help to make this development clear. What other information might be included in the report?

2 blue/yellow   Pupils' book page 27

Children read four short paragraphs of information and decide what kind of report each one comes from and what its purpose is. They then write headings for the paragraphs.

Guided group support

Yellow Help children to focus on the clues in a text that indicate its purpose. Encourage them to identify and note key words. Help children to decide where in a text each paragraph might be situated, and what might come before and after it.

Alternative group activities

blue/yellow   copymaster 8

Children research material to write a related report on the work of the Blue Cross or the RSPCA. They could begin by brainstorming questions they would like to ask, and then refine this down to three main headings (e.g. 'What they do', 'What kind of animals they treat', and 'How they raise money') Following this (possibly for homework), the children could research information to fit these headings, using the internet or other reference sources. (Both the Blue Cross and the RSPCA have websites.) Children can use copymaster 8 to research/plan their report.

yellow   copymaster 8

Children write a similar report to the one modelled in the shared session, based on Keiko the killer whale (see pupil's book p. 19). Children can use copymaster 8 to research/plan their report.

Plenary (1) With children, draw up a 'Non-chronological reports' poster. Use your initial brainstorming notes and add other important points from your shared and independent study sessions.

Shared session (2) ■ Recap the headings suggested for the report in the last shared session ('More about Megan', 'What is wrong with her', 'What she needs').

■ Focus on the 'What is wrong with Megan' section. Brainstorm what you might include in this section, looking back at OHT/poster 8 if necessary:

  ● fleas, mites and lice;
  ● shocked;
  ● underfed.

■ Demonstrate how you can begin the paragraph with a broad statement (e.g. *Megan is in a very poor condition*) which leads into the details.

■ Experiment with three ways of presenting the information:

1 As a **numbered list:**

What is wrong with Megan
Megan is in a very poor condition. She is:

1 infested with fleas, mites and lice
2 shocked
3 underfed

2 As a **bulleted list:**

What is wrong with Megan
Megan is in a very poor condition. She is:

• infested with fleas, mites and lice
• shocked
• underfed

3 Using **subheadings**. These must look different from the main section headings, and introduce more information

What is wrong with Megan
Megan is in a very poor condition.

Fleas, mites and lice
Her fur is full of fleas, mites and lice. They are making her very uncomfortable and her fur is falling out.

Shock
After her 400 mile journey, Megan is very frightened. She won't come out from the corner of her cage.

Lack of food
Megan is very thin. It is clear that she has not eaten for some time.

■ Compare and evaluate these different approaches in terms of clarity, conciseness, and reader appeal.

Group follow-up activities (2) red/blue

Involve all the groups in writing up part of the planned text. Provide differentiation by assigning more or less challenging tasks according to ability.

Guided group support Encourage children to scan the newspaper article to find relevant facts for the 'More about Megan' section and to consider what other information might be included in this section. You could ask them to try presenting this information as a numbered or bulleted list, or with subheadings, as modelled.

Yellow

Children work on the 'What she needs' paragraph.

Guided group support Help children to come up with sensible suggestions as to what this section might include. Refer back to the previous paragraph on 'What is wrong with Megan'. Help children to decide whether to write up the information using bullet points or subheadings.

Alternative group activities **red/blue/yellow**

If children researched the RSPCA or Blue Cross as suggested in the previous shared session, help them to sift the information they have found to select what is most relevant to the headings they have decided upon for their report. (Alternatively, they may agree to change the headings in the light of what they have found.) Ask more able children to consider how they would subdivide this material for presentation using subheadings.
Depending on how much time you wish to devote to this, you could allocate a separate section of the text to each group and ask them to pool their results to produce a complete report, which all children can then comment on.

Plenary (2) Draft the opening statement and closing section together.
If possible, you should now go on to put the whole report together. This will probably be done initially by you and/or children reading out each section in order, but the text should be typed up or written out as soon as is possible thereafter. The class can then evaluate the text and compare it with the journalistic texts previously written. You should then discuss some of the key differences between the two types of text.

Writing clear and cohesive instructions

Objectives To revise the structure and language of instructions

To improve the cohesion of instructions by using linking phrases

To improve the cohesion of instructions by using clear numbering

To use subheadings within a set of instructions

Shared session (1) *You need: OHTs/posters 12 and 13, copymaster 9.*

*This session provides revision of **How to write instructions** (Year 3, Term 2).*

■ Display OHT/poster 12. Tell children that you are going to read a short text and you want them to tell you what kind of text it is (instructions) and to suggest a good title for it (e.g. 'How to get to my house from school').

■ Ask children if anything could be done to make the instructions easier to follow. With prompting if necessary, they should recognise that listing the instructions one below the other would help.

■ Suggest that the instructions could be separated into two sections. Ask children where the break might be. What are each of the two sections about? ('How to find my road' and 'How to find my house'.)

- Display OHT/poster 13. Ask why the title 'HOW TO GET TO MY HOUSE FROM SCHOOL' is in capital letters (it's the **main title**) and 'How to find my road' and 'How to find my house' are in lower case bold letters (they are **subheadings** – less important). Ask whether there are any other ways of highlighting important information (italics, bold, etc.).

- Now look at the language used in each step in the directions, asking children whether they think the text is finished. Could someone really follow these directions easily? Use copymaster 9. Go through the instructions one by one, checking them against the map. Check particularly whether the instructions fit together in a continuous route. Look out for:
  - opportunities to introduce helpful linking words or phrases;
  - any irrelevant information that should be omitted;
  - any helpful information that could be added.

- Here are some suggestions for improvement:

HOW TO GET TO MY HOUSE FROM SCHOOL

How to find my road
Come out of the school gates/ ~~t~~urn right.   *and*

Walk to the corner.

The entrance to the park is on your left.
Cross the road and go into the park, then
~~F~~ollow the path that goes straight ahead.
When you get to the other side of the park,
~~G~~o through the gate/ and

~~Turn left.~~

Take the first road on the right.

You have found my road. Now you have to find my house.

How to find my house
You will see a narrow alley on your right.
Go down the alley until you get to
~~There is~~ a small square of grass.

~~I used to play there when I was very small.~~

Look for the green door/ with

~~Look for the~~ number 22/ on it.

Ring the bell and I will let you in.

You will be very welcome.

- Draw attention to the concluding sentence and discuss its purpose. Can children think of an alternative ending?

Group follow-up activities (1) red/blue/yellow   **Pupil's book page 28**   **copymaster 10**

Children use an instructions framework to plan their own text with two subheadings.

Guided group support

Red Help children to make sure that their instructions are in a logical order and that they do not miss out any stages.

Blue Encourage children to expand their instructions to make them clearer, including extra stages where it may be helpful to the reader

Yellow Encourage children to incorporate a section in the middle which links the two sections (as in the model text).

Plenary (1) Choose two children/pairs/groups who have chosen and planned the same process. Ask the class to see whether the instructions follow the same stages, or whether one includes more stages than the other. Have they missed out anything important?

Shared session (2) ■ Draft the class text using the plan drawn up in the previous shared session.

Group follow-up activities (2) red/blue/yellow

All groups work on drafting from the plan they prepared in the previous session.

Guided group support
Red Remind children to make the main heading and subheadings look different, and to use numbering appropriately.
Blue/Yellow Encourage children to experiment with different ways of linking each sentence to the previous one.

Alternative group activity red/blue/yellow

Each group is given a section of the class text to revise and edit.

Plenary (2) Amend the first draft as fully as possible in the light of suggestions from each group. Then ask children to evaluate these improvements.

Homework suggestions

- Over a week, cut out and collect headlines from different newspapers. Sort them into categories – for example, sensible, funny, dramatic. Choose a favourite and write about why it appeals to you. (**After Session 1**)

- Rewrite these sentences in a sensational, journalistic way. Use a thesaurus and a dictionary to help you. Have fun using exaggerated language! The first one has been done for you as an example:

Cars drive very fast down this quiet street
DEMON DRIVERS TERRORISE PEACEFUL STREET

A house burned down
Firemen rescued a cat from up a tree
Neighbours had an argument
A labrador puppy nearly drowned in the river
A school cook won a prize for serving tasty dinners
Pupils made their own nature garden
A pet snake grew to be the longest in the world
(**After Session 2**)

- Write headlines for traditional tales and nursery rhymes. Try to include rhyme or alliteration in some of your headlines. Here are some headlines for Humpty Dumpty:

IT'S NO YOLK FOR HUMPTY

KING'S MEN SCRAMBLED IN FAILED FIRST AID ATTEMPT

How many headlines can you think of for these?

The Gingerbread Man
Jack and the Beanstalk
Little Bo Peep
Little Red Riding Hood
Little Miss Muffet
The Three Billy-Goats Gruff
(**After Session 2**)

- Choose one of these headlines. Plan a newspaper article to go with it. Use copymaster 7 to make notes.

  The cat that got the cream!
  Disappointment as concert is cancelled
  Motorway dog saved
  Bungling burglar caught red-handed
  Monkey business at the zoo
  (**After Session 3**)

- Choose a recount article from a newspaper or magazine. Make notes in a 'who/what/where/when /why/how' grid like the one in the pupil's book (p. 25). Use these key words to write an attention-grabbing title. Now see how many different summary sentences you can write as the orientation for a newspaper-style recount. To help you, cut up the grid and shuffle the pieces around. Finally, decide on the best orientation. Write it out and draw a picture to go with it. (**After Session 4**)

- Pretend to be a journalist interviewing people about the most exciting or interesting event in their lives. Interview some friends or members of your family. Ask lots of *who, what, where, when, why* and *how* questions. Make notes of what your interviewees tell you. Choose the best story to write up as a recount article for a newspaper. (**After Session 4**)

- Collect front page articles from different newspapers, and paste them into a book. Write which newspaper each one is from, and the date it was published. Write why you think the journalist wrote the article: to tell readers about an important issue, to persuade readers towards a point of view or to entertain readers.

- Write a review of the article you found most interesting or enjoyable, and say why.

UNIT 2 How to write a newspaper-style recount

Colour the right number of stars to show how well you did the following things:

0 stars = I didn't do it.   3 stars = I did it well.

1 star = I gave it a try.   4 stars = I did an excellent job!

2 stars = I did it quite well.

I composed an attention-grabbing headline.	☆	☆	☆	☆
I got all the key details of who, what, where, when and why into my orientation.	☆	☆	☆	☆
All the events in my recount were told in time order with chronological links.	☆	☆	☆	☆
I used powerful language to create a journalistic style.	☆	☆	☆	☆
My caption was short but strong.	☆	☆	☆	☆
I altered my sentences and used a variety of sentences to adapt to a newspaper style.	☆	☆	☆	☆
My reorientation used changing verb tenses to bring it 'up to the minute'.	☆	☆	☆	☆
I wrote an article that provides information and high interest for my readers.	☆	☆	☆	☆

Something I am especially pleased with

Something my audience liked in my writing

Something I'd like to do better next time

Term two fiction focus:
3 How to write a poem about an imagined world

What most children will already know:

That settings can include details of place, time, weather, etc.

How to describe a setting in a prose narrative

That some poems also contain settings

That settings can be real or imaginary

What children will learn in this unit:

How to use language to evoke an imaginary world

How to use similes to help present a fantasy setting

To write poetry based on the style and structure of poems read

How to write a poem with an fantasy setting

---

1 Poems with fantasy settings

Objectives To revise knowledge of settings in narratives

To consider how a fantasy setting is described

Shared session *You need: OHT/poster 14, a large sheet of paper for class poster.*

■ Ask children to think back to their work on settings in stories and poems from Year 3. Recap what children know about settings (e.g. settings tell us where the narrative takes place; they allow the reader to build a picture in his/her imagination; they may include details about place, time of day, period in history, the weather, etc.)

■ Read the first verse of the poem on OHT/poster 14. Ask children what they think the King of Quizzical Island finds at the edge of the world. What sort of settings might there be in this poem?

■ Now read the whole poem. Ask children what they can feel and see in the setting of the poem.

■ Elicit some of the phrases used in the poem to describe the setting. Do children think this is a real setting? Ask what we call a setting that is not real (e.g. **fantasy**).

■ Now show children the poem. Read it again, together. Ask for volunteers to come up and underline the phrases which tell us this is a fantasy setting (e.g. *everything stands on end; rivers go up like fountains; crocodiles stand on their tails*).

■ Ask children if they know any other examples of fantasy settings, in poems, stories, films or computer games. Ask them to describe these settings to you. If necessary, prompt with *Alice in Wonderland* or *Star Wars*. Discuss how these settings are different from realistic ones.

Group follow-up activities **1 red   Pupil's book page 29**

Children look at the imaginary/fantasy scene in the picture. They suggest names for the landscape features. Children then write what they can imagine from this setting.

Guided group support Help children to think of fantastical names for what they see. Encourage them to describe something unusual that might happen in this setting.

2 blue   Pupil's book page 30

Children look at further verses from 'The King of Quizzical Island', and write down the phrases which indicate a fantasy setting. They then write what they can imagine from this setting.

Guided group support Focus on the words that make the setting fantastical or unusual. Using these key words, prompt children to imagine further elements of the setting (e.g. *If the waves are 'as high as hills,' what do you think the fish are like? If the 'blue bits' are sea or sky, what do you think the red bits are?*).

3 yellow   Pupil's book page 31

Children look at another poem and write down the phrases which indicate a fantasy setting. They then write what they can imagine from this setting.

Guided group support As with the blue group, but with specific reference to elements from the alternative text.

Alternative group activity   **red/blue/yellow**

Children think of another imaginary/fantasy setting and draw it, labelling fantasy features.

Plenary   Recap the general points about settings from the shared session. Ask children how the fantasy settings in their activities are different from realistic settings. Make a 'Fantasy poems' poster and write children's answers on this. Keep the poster for subsequent sessions.

Explain that <u>imagination</u> is vital when thinking of and describing fantasy settings, and that children are going to use their imagination when they write their own poems. Finish by asking children to describe the fantasy settings they have drawn.

2 Using similes

Objectives   To introduce similes through a model poem

For children to write their own examples of similes, and use them in their poems

Shared session   *You need: OHT/poster 14, class poster (from Session 1).*

■ Re-read 'The King of Quizzical Island' on OHT/poster 14. Ask children what sort of setting this poem has (fantasy) and how we know this (e.g. because it could not exist in the real world).

■ Explain that the poet, Gordon Snell, has used lots of imagination in this poem. Together, you are going to look at a special way in which writers let other people into their imagination.

■ Underline and read aloud the following line:

The rivers go up like fountains

■ Ask children to describe what they see when they read this. Ask them if they think the rivers are exactly like fountains – the answer is that we do not know, but that the poet has created an image by comparing the rivers to something else. This is called a **simile**.

■ Tell children that there is one other simile in this verse. Ask them to find it. Underline and read it aloud:

> And the meadows tower like mountains

■ Again, ask children if they think the meadows look exactly like mountains. Explain that this is unlikely. Ask children why they think the poet compares meadows to mountains (e.g. because mountains are very tall and the poet is telling us that the meadows are also very tall).

■ Tell children that there is one word which appears in both similes. Ask them for this word (*like*). Explain that when we compare one thing to something else we often use *like*. Ask children to help you complete another simile, such as:

> He jumped like a... (e.g. frog)

■ Now ask children if they know another word, similar to *like* that we use to compare one thing to another (*as*). Explain that when we use *as* in similes, we normally use it twice. Help children to see this by asking them to complete this simile:

> She was as quiet as a... (e.g. mouse)

■ Build up a list of similes that children know or can think of, based on the examples above.

Group follow-up activities

1 red/blue   Pupil's book page 32

Children use words from a prompt box to complete some well-known *like* similes.

Guided group support

Red Brainstorm some more *like* similes. Help children see that some comparisons are more effective than others.

2 red/blue   Pupil's book page 32

Children complete *as* similes to build up a description of a monster. They then draw the monster.

Guided group support

Blue Help children identify a framework for *as* similes. Explain that the usual pattern is:

> as [*adjective*] as a [*noun*]

Encourage children to use this pattern to produce original and interesting similes, which can be made amusing/dramatic/fantastic, etc. as required.

3 yellow   Pupil's book page 33

Children complete more challenging *as* and *like* similes, to form a short descriptive passage. They then read their work aloud to a partner.

Guided group support

As with the blue group. Challenge children to use imaginative or surprising combinations of words. Explain that, for added effect in poetry, alliterative strings of words can be used (e.g. *as yellow as a sinking saffron sun; fizzing like a furious feline*).

Plenary Recap the main points about similes, and add them to the poster which you started in Session 1. It should include the following:

- A simile compares a subject to something else.
- A simile creates an image of what the subject is like.
- Similes can be used with *like* and *as... as*. (*Give two examples here.*)

Ask children for some of the similes they have written in their activities, and add these to the poster.

Ask children why they think fantasy poems might have lots of similes (e.g. because they are about imaginary places and characters, and the poet has to compare these subjects to real things so that readers can form an image of them). Add this point to the poster. Tell children they can use similes in their own fantasy poems to help their readers see their imaginary places.

(3) Style and structure in a poem

Objectives To consider the vocabulary in a model poem (nonsense words and archaic expressions)

To analyse the use of a chorus in the model poem

To revise and extend knowledge of rhyme patterns in poetry

Shared session *You need: OHT/poster 15, 2 different colour OHT pens, OHT/poster 14.*

Because of the length of this poem, you may wish to mask the first verse and focus on the second verse for these points.

- Tell children they are going to hear a new poem. Ask them to close their eyes as you read it, and imagine what is being described. Now read 'The Dong with a Luminous Nose' on OHT/poster 15.

- Ask children what they could see in their 'mind's eye' as the poem was read.

- Ask children what sort of poem they think this is (another fantasy poem). Ask for words and phrases in the poem which tell us this (e.g. *Dong, Jumbly Girl, Oblong Oysters, sky-blue hands, sea-green hair*).

- Focus on the word *Dong*. Is this a real word? Ask children what sort of creature they think a Dong is. Explain that, as well as containing imaginary settings and characters, fantasy poems often contain imaginary, or nonsense, words. This poet, Edward Lear, used lots of nonsense words in his poems.

- Ask children to find other nonsense words in the poem (e.g. *Jumbly*). Underline these words and briefly discuss possible definitions.

- Explain that this poem was written more than a hundred years ago and that some of the language is quite old-fashioned. Ask children for examples of this in the poem, and for the meanings of these words (e.g. *gay* = carefree; *sate* = sat; *for evermore* = always). Underline these words in a different colour.

- Now look at the structure of the whole poem. Ask children how many verses they can see (two). Can they see anything else? Explain that there are four lines at the end of each verse which are the same. Ask if anyone knows what we call this – the answer is in the poem! (The chorus.)

- Explain that many poems and songs have choruses repeated after verses. Ask children why they think this is (e.g. choruses are easy to learn, and allow people to join in parts of the poem, especially when it is being read aloud).

■ Tell children they are going to look at the rhyme scheme in this chorus, to give them a model for writing their own poems.

■ Read the chorus aloud. Underline *few* at the end of the first line in one colour. Ask a volunteer to come up and underline a word that rhymes with *few* (*blue*) in the same colour. Now ask another volunteer to underline the other pair of rhyming words in the chorus (*live; sieve*). With children, work out the rhyme scheme for the chorus. Establish that alternate lines rhyme. Explain this in terms of the colours used to underline the rhyming words (e.g. pink, green; pink, green).

■ Briefly compare this rhyme scheme with that in 'The King of Quizzical Island' on OHT/poster 14. The third verse has exactly the same rhyme scheme as the chorus in 'The Dong...' In the other verses, the first and third lines do not rhyme.

■ Write a new chorus for 'The Dong with a Luminous Nose', using the same rhyme scheme and some of the words of the original, but with new rhyming words. Write this with children, asking them to substitute words where possible – for example:

> Far away, far away,
> Are the woods where the Jumblies walk;
> Their teeth are pink, and their tongues are grey,
> And their favourite food is chalk.

Group follow-up activities

1 red/blue   Pupil's book page 34

Children use the framework provided to write their own choruses for the model poem.

Guided group support

Red Help children with rhyming. Encourage them to try different ways of generating rhyming lines, including starting with a pair of rhyming words and working 'backwards' to fill in the lines.

Blue Work with children to include alliteration and nonsense words, as in the original chorus.

2 red/blue   Pupil's book page 34

Children look at mixed up lines from another poem. They are given the rhyme scheme of the original poem, and write out the poem in the correct order.

3 yellow   Pupil's book page 35

Children use a less restrictive framework to write their own choruses for the model poem. They write two different choruses, using different rhyming words for each one.

Guided group support As with the blue group. Revise what children know about rhythm, and ensure there is strong rhythm in their choruses.

Plenary Recap the features of 'The Dong with a Luminous Nose' that you looked at in the shared session (nonsense words, old-fashioned language, verses and choruses).

Explain that these features occur in different types of poetry, but one feature is particularly associated with fantasy poems. Ask the children which one (nonsense words).

Now ask children to read out their new choruses. Finish by asking them to think of some other poems and songs with choruses.

4 Planning the poem

Objective To involve children in planning their work, and to give them a structure for planning independently

Shared session *You need: OHTs/posters 14 and 16.*

- Briefly recap the setting and events of 'The King of Quizzical Island'. Use OHT/poster 14 if necessary.

- Tell children that they are going to write a poem about another fantasy land which the King of Quizzical Island visits on his travels. Establish the audience for this poem.

- Display OHT/poster 16. Tell children that the poem will have at least four verses, to describe:
  - the journey to the land;
  - what the setting is like;
  - what the king does there;
  - his journey away from this place.

- Together, plan the first verse on OHT/poster 16. Decide whether the king sails up a river or across the sea. What is unusual about the journey? Ask children to think about the size of the waves, the colour of the water, what any creatures look like, etc.

- In the second verse, focus on the setting. Discuss what might make it a fantasy setting – shapes, colours, inhabitants, landscape features, location, etc. Make notes of the key points on OHT/poster 16. For instance, the children might choose:
  - a 'space' setting: two blue suns, purple spiky mountains, orange water in a river;

    or

  - a 'fairy forest' setting: talking trees, a magic stream, a fairy circle.

- Move on to plan the third and fourth verses together. Remind children of the importance of using unusual and intense words, as well as using ordinary words in unusual ways, for description in this poem.

Group follow-up activities

red/blue/yellow

Children use copymaster 11 to plan their own poems.

Guided group support

Red Help children talk about their fantasy settings. Question them closely to make them think about detail. If you wish, restrict this group to three verses: arrival, description and departure.

Blue Help children to consider colour, shape, size, smell, etc. in their descriptions of settings. Challenge them to make something familiar into something fantastical.

Yellow As with the blue group. Encourage children to write an additional verse for the middle of the poem, describing aspects of their fantasy setting, or what the king does there.

Plenary Ask volunteers to describe their plans to the rest of the class. Ask them how they intend to describe their fantasy settings. Can the rest of the class think of words and phrases that might be useful?

⑤ Drafting the poem

Objective   To write poetry based on the structure and style of poems read

Shared session

You need: OHT/poster 16 (from Session 1), large sheets of paper for drafting, 2 different colour marker pens.

*1 See **Drafting** on page 6 for more detailed guidance on conducting a whole-class drafting session.*

2 If you feel children need more support before writing rhyming verses, carry out the drafting over two sessions. In the first, work with children to write out the description and sequence of events in prose; in the second, work to express this in rhyme. You may find that this approach helps to get vocabulary flowing, and prevents children looking for rhymes before focusing on meaning.

■ Revise the structure and rhyme scheme of the class poem, recapping with children what they learnt in Session 3. Establish that this poem, and the children's poems, will have four-line verses and that alternate lines will rhyme.

■ Using your plan on OHT/poster 16, draft the poem with the class.

■ Use alternate colours for the last word of each line. Encourage children to keep to the rhyme scheme – praise the lines they come up with, but remind them that each line will require another line to rhyme with it, later in the verse.

■ Sometimes the writing of a poem will proceed in sequence, adding lines in order. However, children may suggest a line that you think would be better, for example, at the end of the verse. In this case, write it down as line 4, and ask for lines to lead up to it.

Group follow-up activities

red/blue/yellow

Children use their plans to draft their own poems.

Guided group support

Red Support children in working out rhymes for their poems. Help them use a thesaurus to explore different sounding words that mean the same thing. Try out a variety of rhyming possibilities and help them choose the ones that sound best.

Blue As with the red group, but also challenge this group to consider the rhythm of their lines. Help them find longer or shorter phrases and synonyms as required, to add or subtract syllables from lines.

Yellow As with the blue group. Challenge this group to make up some nonsense words.

Plenary   Ask children to read out their draft poems. Divide those listening into two groups, one to imagine the settings being described; the other to listen for the rhyming words. Ask these groups to feed back to the whole class after each poem.

⑥ Revising and editing the poem

Objectives   To write poetry based on the structure and style of poems read

To revise written work and incorporate features of poems with fantasy settings

Shared session   *You need: poem draft (from Session 5), OHTs/posters 14 and 15 (optional).*

*See **Revising and editing** on page 6 for more detailed advice.*

■ Read the draft of the class poem with children. Ask how they think this poem could be improved before publishing it.

- Revise the poetic features which you looked at in the two model poems (unusual descriptions, similes and nonsense words). If necessary, look again at OHTs/posters 14 and 15. Focus on one or more of these features in the class poem.

- Encourage children to look critically at the vocabulary used in the draft. How well do the chosen words describe a fantasy setting? Ask the children to use a thesaurus, or model using one yourself, to find alternative descriptive words.

- When you have finished, ask children to think of a title for the poem.

Group follow-up activities

red/blue/yellow

Children work on revising and editing their own poems.

Guided group support

Red Encourage children to use nonsense words in their poems. Help them use a thesaurus to find descriptive words for their fantasy settings.

Blue/Yellow Encourage children to use interesting similes in their poems, avoiding clichés.

Plenary

Ask children to talk about the changes they have made to their drafts. Ask those listening to comment on how these changes help the description in the poems. Discuss what children have learnt about revising poetry in this session, and how easy or difficult they have found this.

7 Publishing the poem

Objective

To consider the presentational issues involved in writing the final version of a poem

Shared session

You need: a variety of published poems (big book or standard format), revised poem draft, a large sheet of paper, different colour marker pens.

*1 See **Publishing** on page 7 for more detailed notes on the issues involved in the final presentation of the text*

2 Since the poems which children produce independently are usually fairly short, this activity may be a good opportunity to encourage 'best' handwriting.

3 As most of these poems should fit on to one page, you may wish to provide paper with an attractive border for children to write on.

4 Consider whether children should produce two copies of their finished poem: one to be displayed on the classroom wall or collated in a folder for the school library; the other for the child to take home.

- Look at a number of published poems, preferably with a variety of illustrations, borders, etc. Ask the children for similarities in the way these poems are presented.

- Establish that poems are usually written in short lines, instead of going right across the page, and that all lines start with a capital letter – even when it is not the start of a new sentence.

- Now ask children for any differences in the way the poems are presented (e.g. size and number of illustrations, borders, font size, type and use of colour).

- Together, consider how to present the class poem. Make decisions about:
  - illustrations, and how these will show features of the setting(s) in the poem;
  - layout of verses and illustrations on the page;
  - whether the poem should have a border, and how this should be decorated;
  - how you want to write out the poem (in neat handwriting or using a computer), and what colours to use.

Group follow-up activities   **red/blue/yellow**

Children work on publishing their poems.

Guided group support

Red Encourage patience and close attention to detail when children are writing up their neat copies. Help them write out their poems in short lines instead of one continuous text. Make sure that illustrations do not overshadow the poem.

Blue As with the red group. Suggest to children that they 'centre' the lines of text for an attractive effect. Encourage *Wordart* effects on the title of the poem.

Yellow As with the blue group. Confident handwriters may wish to use a 'calligraphy style' to write their poems. Suggest to children that they decorate the first letter in each line, like an old-fashioned manuscript.

Plenary   The children practise reading out their poems to their chosen audience, as well as discussing the presentational choices they have made.

ADDITIONAL SESSIONS

Using expressive language

Objectives   To consider how an imaginary world is described and evoked in a model text

To understand how expressive language can create moods and arouse expectations

For children to write their own examples of expressive language

Shared session   *You need: OHT/poster 17.*

- Tell children you are going to read them a different poem with a fantasy setting. Ask them to close their eyes as you do this, and imagine what is being described. Read 'Jabberwocky' on OHT/poster 17.

- Ask what is special about the poem – establish that it contains lots of nonsense words. Discuss why the poet used nonsense words (e.g. because 'real' words were not unusual enough to describe the setting the poet imagined).

- Read the first verse of the poem again. Ask for volunteers to come up and underline the nonsense words. (Point out that *'Twas* is not a nonsense word but an old-fashioned expression for *It was*.)

- Ask what this first verse is describing – establish that it is about a fantastic setting. Tell children that you are going to go through this verse together and try to describe the setting using real words. These words will have the same number of syllables as the poet's words, to keep the rhythm of the poem.

- Make sure children understand that there are no true meanings of the nonsense words – everyone will have their own ideas.

- Look at *brillig*. Check what children think this means – is it perhaps a time of day? Explain that time of day is often an important aspect of scene-setting. Tell children you need to make the time of day sound like part of the fantasy. This could be done by creating a new compound word. Show the class how to build these – for example, *day-time, night-time, play-time, meal-time, home-time, school-time, fun-time*.

■ Now think of something strange, magical or unusual to add to -*time* (e.g. *spell-time*, *fright-time*, *spook-time*, *grey-time*, *bright-time*). Children's suggestions will be determined by whether they feel the fantasy setting is beautiful, scary or something quite different – for example.

> 'Twas fright-time, and the slithy toves

or

> 'Twas treat-time, and the slithy toves

■ Now establish that *toves* is a **plural noun**, described by the **adjective** *slithy*. First decide what *toves* might be, then choose an appropriate adjective to replace *slithy*. Make sure children understand that their final choices will be partly predetermined by the time of day allocated to *brillig*.

■ Now move on to the words *gyre* and *gimble*. Establish that they are **verbs**. The alternatives you decide on for these will depend on what you chose to replace *slithy toves*, and how children imagine such creatures to move.

■ As you work through the verse, consider rhythm and word-play, such as alliteration, without allowing this to dominate the session.

■ Here are some suggested alternatives to the first verse of 'Jabberwocky':

> 'Twas fright-time, and the poison sands
> Did wail and wobble in the gloom:
> Deep purple were the Martian moons,
> When the dragon eggs hatched out.

or

> 'Twas spelltime, and the golden stars
> Did sing so softly in the dawn:
> Invisible were the talking trees,
> And the rainbow pixies played.

Group follow-up activities

1 red   Pupil's book page 36

Children copy out the first two verses from 'Jabberwocky' in the pupil's book. They identify the nonsense words and choose suitable alternatives from a word bank. They write these alternatives above the nonsense words.

Guided group support Help children identify the nonsense words in the poem, and select the best match for each in the word bank. Encourage them to use a dictionary to check any words they do not know.

2 blue/yellow   Pupil's book page 36

Children write their own version of the first two verses of 'Jabberwocky', using expressive, real alternatives to the nonsense words.

Guided group support

Blue Help children decide what they think each nonsense word means, and encourage them to use a thesaurus to find new and unusual alternatives.

Yellow As with the blue group. Encourage children to make their settings as horrible, funny, frightening or beautiful as possible.

3 red/blue/yellow   Pupil's book page 37

Children copy out a table in the pupil's book. They describe at least one plant, one animal and one type of food in 'this world' and in their 'imagined world'.

Plenary

Children read out their versions of the 'Jabberwocky' verses. Ask the rest of the class to close their eyes as they listen. Ask children whether they think each setting is meant to be horrible, funny, frightening or beautiful.

Writing the poem as a story in chapters

Objectives   To analyse the narrative content of a poem

To plan chapters of a story, using the narrative content of a poem

Shared session   *You need: OHT/poster 17.*

*1 This session should be conducted after the first additional session, **Using expressive language**.*

2 This session focuses on planning a story with chapters. To extend work on writing stories in chapters, conduct a subsequent drafting session using the plans generated here.

■ Recap the setting and details of 'Jabberwocky'. Ask children to tell you what they remember about the place and, although they only looked at the rest of the poem briefly, the characters and the main events.

■ Tell children you are going to look at what happens in each verse of the poem. They are then going to think about what the poem would look like as a story in chapters, and write the plan for this story in their groups. Establish an audience for this plan.

■ Ask children to pay careful attention as you read the poem again. This time, you want them to be aware of what is happening in each verse – where the setting is described, when characters appear, whether there is an issue or a problem that the characters have to deal with, what events take place, etc. Now read the poem on OHT/poster 17.

■ After the reading, focus on the first and final verses. Establish that these are exactly the same – the poem opens by setting the scene, and closes by re-setting it. Ask children why they think this is (e.g. the poet might be showing how things return to 'normal' after the events of the poem). Write *setting the scene* next to these two verses. Explain that no events are featured in this repeated verse. All the characters and events are situated in the five verses in the middle of the poem.

■ Point out that most of the nonsense words appear in the scene-setting verses, and not in the five middle verses. Ask children why they think this is (e.g. because it is important for readers to understand clearly what happens in the main events of the poem).

■ Now go through each verse of the poem, writing notes beside each one. Your notes should look something like this:

     verse 1: scene setting
     verse 2: characters (father and son) discuss problem – monsters
     verse 3: son (hero) seeks monster
     verse 4: monster (Jabberwocky) appears
     verse 5: hero fights and kills monster
     verse 6: characters celebrate resolution of problem
     verse 7: scene re-setting

■ Explain that the five middle verses in the poems are like chapters in a story: each one has a different event which, together, form a whole narrative.

■ Focus on the second verse. If this was a chapter in a story, what might it contain? (e.g. a description of the father and son, of the monsters and the problems they pose). Make notes of these details on the board/flipchart. Ask children what title they would give this chapter.

Group follow-up activities   **red/blue/yellow   Pupil's book page 38   copymaster 12**

Children use copymaster 12 to plan the poem as a story in chapters.

Guided group support

Red Re-read the verses one at a time and discuss their content. Encourage the group to talk freely about how they imagine the basic events could be expanded into the chapters of a story. Draw parallels with any other stories, poems or films children may know.

Blue/Yellow As with the red group, but challenge children to plan their chapters in more detail. Include descriptions of key events and excerpts of dialogue. Try to reproduce the fantasy atmosphere of the poem. Children can write notes in their books if there is not enough space on copymaster 12.

Plenary Volunteers from each group summarise their plans. Encourage the rest of the class to ask questions concerning character and plot details, and whether anything is missing from the plan.

Making notes

Objectives To revise the reasons for note-making

To edit down sentences by deleting less important elements

Shared session *You need: OHT/poster 18.*

■ Revise the reasons for making notes (e.g. for planning written work; to provide information quickly; where there is not enough space to write full sentences).

■ Tell children they are going to write the shortest party invitation ever. Write a standard invitation on the board/flipchart (e.g. *You are invited to a party at my house at 8 o'clock on Saturday*) and ask children to come up and delete words which do not affect the meaning of the invitation.

■ You should be left with:

party my house 8 o'clock Saturday

■ Establish that these words contain all the key information and are quicker to write and read than a full sentence.

■ Now tell children they are going to help the King of Quizzical Island make notes for his ship's logbook. Explain, if necessary, that a logbook is like a ship's diary.

■ Read the letter on OHT/poster 18. Invite children to cross out words and phrases, leaving the key information for the notes. Encourage them to cross out 'small words' such as *an*, *the* and *are*. Discuss why some other words and phrases can be deleted – for example:

  ○ letter greeting and closure – not appropriate for ship's logbook;

  ○ *extraordinary* – extra descriptive detail;

  ○ *just* – extra emphasis.

■ Now write the remaining words in the logbook on OHT/poster 18. It should look something like this:

Visited Vertical Land. Everything stands on end. Rivers like fountains, meadows high as mountains. Crocodiles stand on tails.

■ Emphasise that note-making is meant to save time. Notes should be written as quickly as possible.

Group follow-up activities   **1 red   Pupil's book page 40**

Children write out sentences in note form.

Guided group support Work with children to identify the key words in each sentence.

2 blue/yellow   Pupil's book page 41

Children make notes from a letter, to go in a 'ship's logbook'.

Guided group support

Blue Discuss reasons for deleting words from the full sentences, – for example, extra descriptive detail and extra emphasis.

Yellow As with the blue group. When children have finished, cover up the original letter, and challenge them to turn their notes back into full sentences. Explain that note-making and turning notes back into full sentences are closely connected skills.

Plenary   Ask children to read out the original sentences and passages and the notes they have made from them. Ask the rest of the class to listen carefully for the words and phrases which have been taken out.

Homework suggestions

- Choose some letters of the alphabet. Make up fantastical alliterative phrases that could be included in a poem – for example:

  armed and angry alligaroos

  mouldy maroon mountains

  Use a dictionary for this task. (**After Session 1**)

- Write 'exaggerations' for each of these phrases, to make them describe fantasy settings – for example:

  The mountains were high.

  Exaggeration: *The enormous mountains reached up into space.*

  The river was wide.
  The grass was long and green.
  The ship sailed quickly.
  The monster fought with four swords.
  The king noticed something strange.
  The sun shone brightly.
  Stars twinkled in the dark sky.
  A few flowers were growing nearby.
  The water was deep and cold.
  Large birds flew overhead.

  (**After Session 1**)

- Think of long animal names, like hippopotamus or crocodile. Mix these together to create fantasy creatures, such as crocopotamus or hippodile. Make up as many names as you can. Draw two of your favourites and write short descriptions of their behaviour. (**After Session 1**)

- Make choruses from simple phrases. Follow these steps:

  1 Think of a place and a feature of its setting, then think of an adjective to describe it – for example, *Wobblyland, water* and *wild.*

  2 Make these into a simple phrase – for example, *Wild was the water of Wobblyland.*

  3 Now experiment by adding in some simple adjectives to make a repetitive phrase:

  Wet and wild
  Deep and wild
  Dark and wild
  Wild was the water of Wobblyland.

  (**After Session 3**)

- The King of Quizzical Island goes to Jigsaw Land. Can you think of any other toy worlds he could visit? How about Building Block Land, where he might have to build himself somewhere to stay during his visit? Invent another toy world, and write about what the king does there. (**After Session 3**)

- Choose an ordinary scene and write four short sentences to describe it. For instance, a beach scene may look like this:

  The sky was blue. The sea was calm. The sand was dry and golden. The sun shone brightly.

  Now rewrite the description as a fantasy setting. It may help if you use some opposite meanings and move the words around in each sentence:

  Red was the sky. The sea was dry. The shining sands poured like gold. Darkly sang the sun above.

  (After Additional session 1)

- Think of some ordinary landscape features and describe them in this chart. Now think how to make them fantastical.

Feature	Normal description	Fantastical description
a river	*flowing downhill, wet*	*flowing uphill, dry as dust*

(After Additional session 1)

- Draw a picture of a crazy, fantasy place and the people or animals that live there. Invent names for some of them. Write a glossary to go with your picture.

- Talk to a friend about what you might find in the following fantasy places:

  The Upside-down empire
  Back-to-front village
  Stay-awake city
  Lazy land
  Angry avenue
  Silly street
  Zany zoo

  Write a short description of two of these places.

UNIT **3** How to write a poem about an imagined world

Colour the right number of stars to show how well you did the following things:

0 stars = I didn't do it.   3 stars = I did it well.
1 star = I gave it a try.   4 stars = I did an excellent job!
2 stars = I did it quite well.

I used my imagination and my experience of books and films to create a fantasy world.	☆	☆	☆	☆
I used details and powerful language to describe my imaginary setting.	☆	☆	☆	☆
I used alliteration, onomatopoeia and other word-play to make my poem enjoyable.	☆	☆	☆	☆
I wrote using a verse structure and rhyme scheme.	☆	☆	☆	☆
I used similes to help describe my setting, events or characters.	☆	☆	☆	☆
I managed the rhythm of my poem by counting syllables.	☆	☆	☆	☆
I managed the beat of my poem by thinking about stressed and unstressed syllables.	☆	☆	☆	☆
I used short lines and strong ideas to create something very different from a story.	☆	☆	☆	☆

Something I am especially pleased with

Something my audience liked in my writing

Something I'd like to do better next time

Term two non-fiction focus:
4 How to write an explanation of a process

What most children will already know:

That explanations are used to give information

That explanations often refer to <u>how</u> and <u>why</u> things happen

Basic features of instruction texts (steps in chronological sequence)

Basic features of report texts (impersonal style, written in present tense, detailed information and technical vocabulary)

What children will learn in this unit:

How explanations differ from instructions

Some similarities and differences between explanations and reports

To promote cohesion in explanations by the careful use of appropriate connectives

To apply a known range of chronological connectives to support sequential explanations

To learn and use a range of causal connectives

To use paragraphs to structure and clarify written explanations

To use paragraph sub-headings to label content and further clarify structure

 Looking at an explanation

Objectives   To establish the purpose of an explanation

To investigate the similarities and differences between an explanation text and instructions and reports

Shared session   *You need: OHT/poster 19, a large sheet of paper for class poster.*

■ Read 'Cleaning water' on OHT/poster 19. Ask children for the **purpose** of this text (e.g. it tells us how and why water is cleaned).

■ Explain that this text is an **explanation of a process**. Discuss briefly other processes children can think of (e.g. the water cycle, recycling paper or glass).

■ Focus on the second paragraph. Point out that this explanation contains a sequence of steps. Ask children to identify and underline these steps (see below).

■ Ask what other texts have steps in sequence (instructions). Recap that instruction texts show the reader how to make or do something – check if this text instructs us to do something (not directly).

■ Point out that explanation texts contain **detailed information**, often with **technical vocabulary**. Identify and underline an example on the OHT/poster (see below).

■ Explanations are also written in an **impersonal style**, usually in the **present tense**. Again, identify and underline examples (see below).

■ Ask what other texts often have these features of detailed information, technical vocabulary, present tense and impersonal style (reports).

- Revise that most reports are non-chronological – the information is not in a sequence of steps. Check whether this text is non-chronological (no – look at the steps you have already underlined).

Cleaning water

The importance of clean water
detailed information → Water is essential for life. It is needed for drinking, as well as washing, cooking and many industrial processes. After it is used, however, water is often dirty and contaminated. For this reason, the process of cleaning water is very important.

Making fresh water clean enough to drink
sequence of steps → Water from rivers and lakes is pumped to a reservoir. Then it goes to a treatment works. It is held in tanks so that any soil or dirt sinks to the bottom. Next, the water is passed through very fine filters that leave it completely clear. So that the water is also free of invisible bacteria, chemicals are added afterwards. Lastly, it is pumped to taps.

Cleaning up used water
When it is flushed away, dirty water is carried along a drainage system to a sewage works. Immediately, paper, plastic and other materials are sieved out. Then the sewage is held in settlement tanks so that solid matter settles as sludge, and can be taken out. The remaining liquid is
impersonal style → passed through filters in order to remove pollution. Finally, the water is clean enough to release back into rivers and seas.

The importance of recycling water
present tense → The Earth's water is very old and is constantly recycled by natural processes. However, this planetary hydrological cycle cannot cope with
technical vocabulary → the high levels of water pollution produced by humans. Governments are introducing environmental protection laws, which demand efficient water-cleaning processes to protect the planet's water.

Group follow-up activities

1 red   Pupil's book page 42

Children use a simplified version of 'Cleaning water'. They find further examples of explanation text features.

Guided group support Focus on the three most characteristic features of the text: present tense, steps in chronological order, details of <u>how</u> and <u>why</u> things happen.

2 blue   Pupil's book page 43

As for activity 1, using a more challenging text.

Guided group support As with the red group. Highlight examples of technical vocabulary.

3 blue   Pupil's book page 43

Children think of two differences between an explanation text and a set of instructions.

4 yellow   Pupil's book page 44

As for activity 1, using a more challenging text.

Guided group support Focus on the formal, impersonal style of the text.

5 yellow   Pupil's book page 44

Children think of two differences between an explanation text and

- a set of instructions
- a non-chronological report.

Plenary   Make an 'Explanations' poster. Write up all the points children have learnt so far about explanations.

- They tell us about a process.
- They present information in a sequence of steps, but do not tell us directly how to do something.
- They contain a lot of detailed information.
- They often contain technical vocabulary.
- They are usually written in the present tense.
- They are written in an impersonal style.

2 The structure of an explanation text

Objectives   To understand how explanation texts are organised

To consider how sub-headings help the organisation of the text

Shared session   *You need: OHT/poster 19, strips of paper (see below), class poster (from Session 1).*

If necessary, revise paragraphing. Recap that:
- *a paragraph is a section of writing in a text, separated by a space or indent;*
- *it contains a number of sentences about the same idea, event or sequence;*
- *it should make sense on its own and as part of a whole text.*

■ Recap on the features of explanation texts from Session 1. Tell children you are going to see how an explanation text is organised.

■ Draw boxes around the title and the paragraphs on OHT/poster 19.

■ Ask children to help you identify the role of each section in the text. Firstly, identify and mark the title. Revise the importance of informative titles for all kinds of text

■ Look at the first paragraph. Ask children what it is (the opening section). What does it tell us? (why we need clean water) Establish that an explanation of a process usually begins with an opening section, which gives a reason for the process. Write *opening section – reason for process* next to this paragraph.

■ Look at the second and third paragraphs. Ask what job they do (they explain the process of cleaning water). Each paragraph deals with a different part of the process. Ask children to tell you what these parts are (before/after or clean/dirty). Recap on the sequence of steps in each of these paragraphs. Write *explanation of the process* alongside both paragraphs.

■ Look at the last paragraph. Ask children what it is (the closing section). Ask what job it does (it gives us more information about cleaning water). Point out that an explanation text usually ends with a closing section. This adds to the information given in the introduction. Write *closing section – additional information* next to this paragraph.

■ Now look at the **sub-headings** in the text. Ask children what job these do (they tell us what is in each paragraph). Cover up the sub-headings with strips of paper. Ask if the structure of the text is still clear. Explain that, without sub-headings, we need to read a text more carefully to see how it is organised. Sub-headings provide <u>instant access</u> into a text.

- With the sub-headings still covered, ask children to think of alternative sub-headings – for example:

  paragraph 1: Why clean water is needed
  paragraph 2: How to clean fresh water
  paragraph 3: How to clean used water
  paragraph 4: Why water has to be recycled efficiently

- Compare these sub-headings with the originals. Discuss with the children that there are **key words** in the text which we need to use in most of the sub-headings (*water, clean*).

Group follow-up activities

1 red/blue   Pupil's book page 45   copymaster 13

Children read the 'Recycling glass bottles' text, and draw boxes around the opening section, explanation and closing section. They then match sub-headings to the appropriate paragraph.

Guided group support

Red Support children in identifying the main content of each section and the associated key words. Demonstrate the link between these key words and the same words in the sub-headings.

2 blue   Pupil's book page 45   copymaster 13

Children decide which sentences in the pupil's book should go with which paragraph on the copymaster.

Guided group support Help children identify and mark the content and key words in the additional sentences. Help find similar content and vocabulary in the text on the copymaster.

3 yellow   Pupil's book page 45   copymaster 14

As for activity 1, using a more challenging text ('Making compost')

Guided group support Ensure use of impersonal language in sub-headings. You may wish children to write their initial suggestions on a whiteboard first, for consideration by the group. Demonstrate different ways of eliminating personal language.

4 yellow   Pupil's book page 45   copymaster 14

As for activity 2, using the 'Making compost' text.

Plenary   Return to your 'Explanations' poster. Recap the structure of explanations. Recap how sub-headings help the organisation of the text. Add these points to the poster.

(3) Using chronological connectives

Objectives   To revise chronological connectives and establish their importance in explanation texts

To make short notes by completing a flow-chart

Shared session   *You need: OHT/poster 19, OHT/poster 20, class poster (from Session 2).*

- Recap what children have learnt about explanation texts. Revise the point that the actual explanation of the process follows a sequence of steps.

■ Ask for some words which tell us when things happen in a sequence (e.g. *first, then*). Brainstorm some more of these (e.g. *before, afterwards, next, finally*). Explain that these time words are called **chronological connectives**.

■ Ask children to identify and underline the chronological connectives on OHT/poster 19 (*then, next, afterwards, lastly, immediately, then, finally*). Discuss how these establish the order of each step in the sequence.

■ Try reading part of the text aloud, omitting the underlined words. Discuss how this makes the explanation more difficult to understand.

■ Use OHT/poster 20. Establish that the text above the flow-chart is the second paragraph from 'Cleaning water'. With the children, write out the process in the flow-chart. Write in notes – for example:

1 water pumped to reservoir ⟶
2 held in tanks in treatment works – soil/dirt sinks to bottom ⟶
3 water passed through filters ⟶
4 chemicals added to get rid of invisible bacteria ⟶
5 water pumped to taps

■ Now ask children to find chronological connectives from the text, and fill them into the appropriate space next to each box. Establish that there is no connective in the text for the first box – move straight on to the second box and come back to this later. Write *then, next, afterwards* and *lastly* underneath the appropriate boxes. Now come back to the first box and ask for a suitable connective here (e.g. *firstly, first of all*).

Group follow-up activities

1 red   Pupil's book page 46   copymaster 15

Children write a shortened version of recycling glass bottles as a flow-chart on copymaster 15. They choose chronological connectives from a list and add these to the correct stages of the flow-chart.

Guided group support Work with children to select an appropriate connective for each part of the flow-chart.

2 blue/yellow   Pupil's book pages 46–47   copymaster 15

Children look at pictures and captions illustrating the chocolate-making process. They write this out as a flow-chart on copymaster 15, adding chronological connectives at the appropriate stages.

Guided group support

Blue Help children to write notes rather than full sentences.

Yellow Help children to identify that words like *next* and *then* are often over-used. Work with them to find suitable synonyms in a thesaurus.

3 red/blue/yellow   Pupil's book page 47   copymaster 15

Children write out another process as a flow-chart (on a clean copy of copymaster 15). Here are some ideas for processes: the life-cycle of a frog or butterfly; the water cycle; other recycling processes (e.g. aluminium or plastic), electrical circuits.

Plenary Return to your 'Explanations' poster. Ask why it is important to use chronological connectives in the explanation of a process (e.g. they keep the steps of a process in the correct sequence). Add this to the poster. Ask for examples of chronological connectives children have used in their activities. Write these on the poster.

(4) Using causal connectives

Objective To investigate the function and importance of causal connectives in explanation texts

Shared session *You need: OHT/poster 19, class poster (from Session 3).*

*To make the use of causal connectives clear, we describe the parts of the sentence they link as **action** and **reason**.*

■ Start by asking children why water needs to be cleaned (e.g. because it may be dirty; to get rid of germs; so that it can be drunk). Write this up as a sentence on the board/flipchart, for example:

> Water is cleaned because it may contain harmful bacteria.

■ Demonstrate that this sentence contains two parts, linked by a connective:

Action:	Water is cleaned
Connective:	because
Reason:	it may contain harmful bacteria.

■ Recap that explanation texts are about <u>why</u> as well as <u>how</u> a process happens. Explain that they usually contain sentences which describe an action and the reason for it, linked by a connective.

■ Identify and underline examples of these sentences on OHT/poster 19. Ask children to divide these sentences into their two parts, identifying the connective used – for example:

Action:	It is held in tanks
Connective:	so that
Reason:	any soil or dirt sinks to the bottom.

Action:	The remaining liquid is passed through filters
Connective:	in order to
Reason:	remove pollution.

■ Return to your original sentence on the board/flipchart. Establish the order of this sentence – action, connective, reason. Explain that we can emphasise the reason by putting it before the action. Reorder the first sentence with the class (*Because it may contain harmful bacteria, water is cleaned*). Point out that the connective now goes at the beginning, and that you have added a comma to separate the purpose from the action.

■ Ask children to find a sentence in this order on the OHT/poster:

Connective:	So that
Reason:	the water is also free of invisible bacteria,
Action:	chemicals are added afterwards.

Group follow-up activities **1 red/blue**   **Pupil's book page 48**

Children identify action, reason and the connective in sentences about paper recycling.

Guided group support

Red Help children to identify which part of the sentence is action and which reason. Ask questions about the action (e.g. *why do we do...?*) so that they can see the reason.

2 red   Pupil's book page 49

Children write sentences of their own using causal connectives. (Specify how many you want them to write.)

3 blue   Pupil's book page 49

Children write five sentences of their own using causal connectives.

Guided group support Encourage the use of a thesaurus to find alternative causal connectives.

4 yellow   Pupil's book page 49

Children read a short explanation about recycling paper. They link short sentences together with causal connectives.

Guided group support Encourage sentences which introduce the reason before the action, as well as vice versa. Discuss which sentences are more suited to having the reason introduced before the action.

5 yellow   Pupil's book page 49

As for activity 3.

Plenary Return to your 'Explanations' poster. Recap the points from the shared session and add these to the poster. You should include the following:

- Connectives link action and reason together in a sentence. They can make short sentences longer, and more natural-sounding.
- If the action goes before the reason, it is linked by the connective.
- If the reason goes before the action, the connective goes at the start of the sentence, and a comma separates the action from the reason.

Brainstorm a list of causal connectives used in the activities, and add this to the poster.

5 Planning the explanation

Objectives To identify audience and purpose for writing explanation texts

To use the organisation and features of a model text to plan new explanation texts

Shared session *You need: a large sheet of paper, OHT/poster 21.*

For a cross-curricular link, explanations could be about the following processes:
- *glass, paper or aluminium recycling (geography);*
- *filtering, melting or evaporating (science);*
- *how electrical circuits work; how musical instruments are made; how textile containers are made (design and technology).*

- Tell children they are going to plan and write their own explanations of a process. Identify the audience and purpose for writing. Decide how the work will be published (e.g. in a small book, as a poster, on a website).

- Decide on the process for the class explanation text. Brainstorm technical vocabulary that may be required. Write this on a poster, as a word bank for later sessions.

- Use the planning framework on OHT/poster 21. Make it clear that you do not have to keep to the exact number of paragraphs on the framework.

- First agree on and note the key points to go in the opening section. Decide the reason(s) for the process. Discuss whether additional information should be provided, and add further notes if required.

- Then talk through the whole of the process. Ask children to list the steps of the process and ensure that they are in correct sequence. Decide how many paragraphs will be required – does each step require a paragraph of its own, or do some steps go together?

■ Discuss what should go in the closing section – this should be extra information about the process.

■ Finally, discuss whether the class text will feature a diagram. If you do have a diagram, decide whether it will illustrate all, or part of, the process. Make notes about this on your planning framework.

■ Read through the plan again and ensure that it makes sense and contains all the necessary key points.

Group follow-up activities

1 red   Pupil's book page 50

Children use the frame in the pupil's book to plan their explanation texts.

Guided group support Involve children in brainstorming and organising content.

2 blue/yellow   Pupil's book page 51

Children use the frame in the pupil's book to plan their explanation texts.

Guided group support

Blue Prompt detailed brainstorming. Challenge children to extend or adapt the framework as appropriate to their material, purpose and audience.
Yellow Challenge children to draw up their own framework.

Plenary   Ask the guided group and one other group to evaluate their plans. Did they experience any particular problems or successes?

6 Drafting the explanation

Objective   To draft an explanation text, working from a plan

Shared session   *You need: OHT/poster 21, word bank (from Session 5), class poster (from Session 4).*

*See **Drafting** on page 6 for more detailed advice on conducting a whole-class drafting session.*

■ Revise the class plan for your explanation text. Revise also the purpose and audience for writing.

■ Refer to the brainstormed vocabulary list and your 'Explanations' poster. Decide on appropriate language to use in the text.

■ Draft the text, keeping to the plan. Encourage children to use impersonal language. If this is difficult, 'convert' their suggestions as you work, both speaking aloud and writing out the impersonal form.

■ When you write the steps of the process, ask children for appropriate chronological connectives.

■ To encourage children to think of causal connectives, ask them why each step in the process is necessary. Try to vary the connectives used here, but do not worry too much about placing the reason before the action – this can be a revising focus.

■ Ask children to think of simple sub-headings for each paragraph. These should be simple 'headlines' of content, to be expanded in the revising session.

Group follow-up activities

red/blue/yellow

Children draft their own explanation texts.

Guided group support

Red Help children to get their writing flowing during a 'try-it-out' session using whiteboards.

Blue Use whiteboards as with the red group. Focus on the type and length of sentences, including the use of connectives.

Yellow Encourage children to write in an impersonal style, using objective language.

Plenary

Ask the guided group and one other group to contribute their thoughts on progress so far. Ask these children to read the parts of their text they consider successful.

---

(7) Revising and editing the explanation

Objectives

To read back written work with a view to improving it

To ensure inclusion of the features looked at in the model text

Shared session

You need: explanation draft, class poster (from Session 4).

*See **Revising and editing** on page 6 for more detailed advice.*

- ■ Briefly revise paragraphing (see the note on p. 80 if necessary). Read through the draft and ask children to help you look for any paragraphs which can be improved.

- ■ Look at the sub-headings used in the draft. Can these be improved in any way? Recap that sub-headings usefully summarise the contents of each paragraph, and often repeat the key words in an explanation text.

- ■ Ask children to identify the chronological connectives. Underline these. Are more needed to help the audience understand the sequence of steps? Can better synonyms be substituted? Refer to your 'Explanations' poster.

- ■ Now identify and underline the causal connectives. Can you vary the connectives used? Again, use your 'Explanations' poster.

- ■ Are there any examples where the reason should be emphasised before the action? If so, revise that the connective goes at the start of the sentence, and that a comma is required to separate the reason from the action.

Group follow-up activities

red/blue/yellow

Children work on revising their explanation texts.

Guided group support

Red Focus on the clarity of the children's texts. Children read their work aloud to a partner who listens for over-long sentences and sections where the meaning is not clear.

Blue As with the red group. Focus on connectives. Have these been used to best effect?

Yellow Concentrate on the formal tone and style. Ensure subject-specific vocabulary has been used appropriately. Identify and take out any personal or conversational language.

Plenary   Ask children for amendments and improvements they have made to their texts. Volunteers read aloud passages of text which they feel need improvement. Ask the rest of the class to respond with a range of constructive comments and suggestions.

8   Publishing the explanation

Objectives   To consider presentational issues

To ensure that the text reaches its target audience

Shared session   *You need: revised explanation draft, different colour marker pens, computer and word-processing software (optional).*

*See **Publishing** on page 7 for more detailed notes on the issued involved in the final presentation of the text.*

- Write out or print out the final version of the explanation.

- Emphasise the importance of a formal presentational style for this type of text.

- Decide on an appropriate page layout, taking into account whether, and where, any diagrams should be incorporated. If you planned a diagram in Session 5, this is an opportunity to draw it or to incorporate one from another source.

- Decide how to present the title and headings, using different font-sizes, types and/or colour, as well as different highlighting effects, such as bold or underlining. Encourage children to consider the needs of the audience when making these decisions.

- Decide whether to present technical vocabulary in italics or some other highlighting effect.

Group follow-up activities   **red/blue/yellow**

Children work on the presentation of their explanation texts.

Guided group support

Red Suggest that the main title is presented in capital letters and the sub-headings are underlined, or use alternative means of highlighting both differently. Help children situate their diagram close to the section of text which it illustrates. Consider how to arrange text around or alongside the diagram.

Blue As with the red group. Consider alternative layouts, for example paragraphs placed asymmetrically or text flowing around diagrams.

Yellow As with the blue group. Include use of italics or other highlighting effect for subject specific vocabulary. If there is time, challenge children to add a glossary to their text.

Plenary   Ask children to explain decisions they have made in producing the final copy of their explanation texts. Finished texts can be shared with the rest of the class, who contribute an 'audience response'.

ADDITIONAL SESSIONS

 ## More about making notes

Objectives   To identify key words in a text

To make short notes

Shared session   *You need: OHT/poster 22, different coloured OHT pens.*

■ Display and read OHT/poster 22 to the class. Ask children what sort of text this is (an explanation of a process). Identify the subject (wool-making) and purpose (explaining how wool is made).

■ Tell children they are going to make notes from this text. Explain that the first stage in making notes is to identify the key words in a text.

■ Look at the first paragraph. Ask children to volunteer words they think are important. Encourage them to think about the subject and purpose of the text as they do this. Underline the key words.

■ Now explain that the second stage is to take out all the other words which are not essential to the meaning. Ask which words you can cross out – encourage children to be ruthless!

■ If any words remain, without being crossed out or underlined, decide whether they are important or not. Do they tell us about the subject or purpose of the text, or are they just 'supporting' words?

■ Write out the first paragraph in note form. Discuss using symbols instead of words – for example, = instead of *made from*. Your notes may look like this:

> Wool = fibres from fleece of sheep. Sheep farmed for wool.
> $\frac{1}{2}$ world's wool from Australia and N.Z.

■ Check that your notes contain all the key information in the text.

■ Repeat this process with another paragraph. Making notes on the third and fourth paragraphs is given as a follow-up activity, so you may want to stick to the first two paragraphs here, or include the fifth paragraph as well.

Group follow-up activities   **1 red   Pupil's book page 52**

Children write out sentences on wool-making as notes.

Guided group support Work with children to identify the key words in each sentence.

 2 red   Pupil's book page 52

Working with a partner, children write three new sentences. They then write them as notes.

3 blue/yellow   Pupil's book page 53

Children write out two paragraphs from the wool-making text as notes.

Guided group support

Blue Help children to keep their notes as brief as possible.

Yellow As with the blue group. Encourage children to experiment with making notes in different ways, such as flow-charts.

4 blue/yellow   Pupil's book page 53

As for activity 3 but writing five sentences.

Plenary   Identify the importance of note-making for a variety of purposes. Discuss how identifying key words can help us search for information – for example, in book indexes or on the internet.

Writing up from notes

Objectives   To reconstruct meaning using key words

To write connected prose from key words

Shared session   *You need: OHT/poster 22, OHT/poster 23.*

■ Recap what children learnt about making notes in the previous session. Explain that it is also important to be able to write full sentences from notes.

■ Display OHT/poster 23. Elicit that these are notes made from the first three paragraphs of the wool-making text.

■ Discuss whether the meaning is clear in the notes. Draw attention to the way different information is recorded on separate lines. Recap how symbols may be written in words, for instance = can stand for *is*.

■ Work with children to turn the notes into full sentences and paragraphs. Explain that it is not necessary to recreate the exact wording of the original text, but the meaning should be the same. Try out some different sentence ideas for each note, then compose the text together.

■ Compare the new version to the original, on OHT/poster 22. Discuss differences and similarities.

Group follow-up activities   **1 red/blue   Pupil's book page 54**

Children swap with a partner the notes they made in the previous session and write them out as full sentences.

Guided group support

Red Discuss with children what the note-form information means to them. Encourage them to construct simple sentences, as close as possible to the basic form of the notes themselves.

Blue Identify key words that should be reproduced without change, but otherwise encourage substitution of synonyms to improve the sentences.

2 yellow   Pupil's book page 54

Children write notes, taken from the wool-making text, as full sentences.

Guided group support   As with the blue group, but also ask children to attempt a formal style.

3 blue/yellow   Pupil's book page 54

Children match notes to the sentences they were made from.

Plenary   All groups contribute examples of sentences written from notes. Discuss any problems or difficulties encountered. Compare these sentences with the original ones in the pupil's book (on pp. 50 and 51). Is the meaning still the same?

Presenting information from different sources

Objectives   To integrate information from a variety of sources

To display information in one simple format

To incorporate diagrams, illustrations and annotations

Shared session   *You need: a large sheet of paper for wall chart, scissors, glue.*

■ It is essential that children do the following as homework before this session:

- Divide the class into three groups. Each child receives a copy of copymaster 16. Assign one of the materials on copymaster 16 to each group – it is best if they research materials which they have not already looked at in this unit (i.e. plastic bottles, drinks cans and clothes).
- Explain that children must research answers for their material. They can work independently or as a group.
- Point out the difference between **recycling** (making new material from something already used) and **reusing** (using something again, or giving it to someone else to use).
- Suggest sources the children can use in their research: information books, encyclopaedias and websites.
- Ask children to find useful diagrams and illustrations for their material.

■ Copy out the chart on copymaster 16 on to a large sheet of paper, to be used as a wall chart. Leave space for diagrams.

■ Ask groups for the information they have collected and fill in the chart. Ask children to help you write this information in note form.

■ Check that the presentation looks attractive and is easy to read.

■ Identify which points would most benefit from an annotated diagram or illustration, and where these could go on the chart. If children have prepared/found illustrations and diagrams, these can be cut out and stuck up here. Alternatively, ask children to help you draw some illustrations or diagrams.

Group follow-up activities   **1 red/blue/yellow   Pupil's book page 55   copymaster 16**

Assign one of the remaining materials on copymaster 16 to the three groups. As before, children research information from a variety of sources.

2 red/blue/yellow   Pupil's book page 55

Children think of diagrams and/or illustrations to accompany their material. Ideas for these are given in the pupil's book.

Guided group support   Identify the key words in the information children have found. Make sure children recognise that these same key words are appropriate for labelling diagrams. Help children copy or draw an appropriate picture, then label it clearly.

Plenary   Add the new information (text and diagrams) to the wall chart. Display it prominently in class.

Homework suggestions

- Change a simple set of instructions (e.g. a recipe) into an explanation of a process. Remember to include an opening section, an explanation of the process and a closing section. (**After Session 1**)

- Look at another explanation text. Use copymaster 15 to work out the plan of this text. (**After Session 2**)

- Choose a process from the list below, or choose another subject. Find out as much as you can about the process. Use topic books, encyclopaedias or the internet. Pretend you are writing for an alien, so you have to explain everything in detail. Remember to write an explanation, not a set of instructions!
  - the life-cycle of a frog or butterfly
  - the water cycle
  - how an electrical circuit works
  - how plastic or aluminium is recycled
  (**After Session 2**)

- Look at the process you wrote about after Session 2. Draw a flow-chart to show this process. (**After Session 3**)

- Find synonyms for *then*. Think of a sentence using each one. (**After Session 3**)

- Listen to explanations on the television and radio. Write down any words or phrases that are commonly used in them. Make a list of the connectives used. (**After Session 4**)

- Use copymaster 16. Your teacher will tell you which material to research. Find information to answer the questions about your material. Use encyclopaedias, information books, and the internet. (**Before 'Presenting information from different sources'**)

- Cut out as many explanation texts as you can find over the course of a week in newspapers, magazines... even comics! Stick these on to larger sheets of paper and write where each one comes from. Make up a class folder of explanations.

UNIT 4 How to write an explanation of a process

Colour the right number of stars to show how well you did the following things:

0 stars = I didn't do it.   3 stars = I did it well.
1 star = I gave it a try.   4 stars = I did an excellent job!
2 stars = I did it quite well.

I kept all the steps of the process in sequence.	☆	★	☆	☆
I used chronological connectives to keep the sequence clear.	☆	☆	☆	☆
I used causal connectives effectively.	☆	☆	☆	☆
I used the correct technical vocabulary for the subject.	☆	☆	☆	☆
I started my writing with a clear definition.	☆	☆	☆	☆
I gave enough supporting information to help my readers to understand the process.	☆	☆	☆	☆
I used paragraphs and headings to keep the text organised.	☆	☆	☆	☆
I included a clear, informative diagram.	☆	☆	☆	☆

Something I am especially pleased with	Something my audience liked in my writing

Something I'd like to do better next time

Term three fiction focus:
5 How to write a story in chapters

What most children will already know:

That stories are shaped and sequenced into a basic beginning, middle and end structure

That stories contain events, characters, settings and dialogue

That stories must be crafted to appeal to and entertain the intended audience

That authors often divide longer stories into chapters

That chapters link together into a whole story like episodes in a series

What children will learn in this unit:

That many stories incorporate a theme that underlies the subject matter

That many themes relate to real-life issues

To develop familiar short story planning techniques for writing longer stories

To use chapters to establish control of longer stories

To write a story about a real-life issue, and develop this through events and interaction between characters

To provide interesting details in each chapter to make the story entertaining and varied

To incorporate links between chapters to maintain continuity and encourage reader interest

To present longer texts attractively

---

① Using chapters to organise longer stories

Objectives
To review what is already known about planning and organising stories

To consider how chapters help organise longer stories

To investigate the value of chapter headings

Shared session
You need: OHT/poster 24, OHT/poster 25, a large sheet of paper for class poster.

*Children may wish to read Michael Morpurgo's **Red Eyes at Night** (Hodder Children's Books, 1998) for themselves.*

■ Revise story structure. Refer back to **How to write a historical story** (pp. 24–37 of this book). Recap that stories should have:
- ○ clear, interesting beginnings, with details of setting, character and a problem;
- ○ a series of events in the middle section, which lead on from each other;
- ○ a climax in the middle section;
- ○ a resolution to the problem in the ending;
- ○ new paragraphs for new events and changes of time/place.

■ Establish that authors use a similar structure for longer stories and novels. Explain that we can use chapters to organise longer stories into clear sections, just as we use paragraphs to organise shorter pieces of writing. Discuss any stories in chapters you have recently read together.

■ Tell children you are going to look at how chapters are used in a novel called *Red Eyes at Night* by Michael Morpurgo. Given this title, can children predict what the book is about? Can they suggest what type of story it might be (e.g. horror story, traditional tale, contemporary story)?

- Display OHT/poster 24. Ask what it is (a contents page) and where you would expect to find it (at the beginning of a book). Explain that each chapter has a title, and that the first page number of each chapter is listed. Point out that chapters do not always have titles: sometimes they are simply numbered. Elicit the purpose of this contents page (e.g. it tells us where to find each chapter, and what each one is called).

- Ask children if they can predict what happens in the story from these chapter titles. Discuss possible suggestions. Who do they think *Little Toad* might be? Are there any clues about who is telling the story (the author or a narrator – look at the chapter title 'My Grand Plan')? Identify that the titles are more 'chatty' and amusing than informative.

- Explain that the author wrote a plan for this story, just as the children will do for their stories. Display OHT/poster 25 and tell children that Michael Morpurgo's plan probably looked something like this.

- Read the plan aloud. Check if any predictions about the type of story, and what happens, were correct.

- Box the first and final chapters separately, then box the remaining chapters together. Elicit that this is the familiar beginning, middle and end framework children have used to structure their shorter stories.

- Count the chapters that make up the middle section – there are six. Discuss the difference between this plan and one for a shorter story (the middle section has been expanded). Explain that this difference is a key feature of longer stories.

- Tell children their next writing project will be to write a story in chapters.

Group follow-up activities

1 red/blue   Pupil's book page 56   copymaster 17

Children read a contents list of chapters and discuss what they think happens in the story. They decide how these chapters fit into the beginning, middle and end framework on copymaster 17. They write planning notes for each chapter in the framework. Finally, they think of a suitable title for the story.

Guided group support

Red Help children understand that these chapter headings <u>summarise</u> what happens in each chapter. Prompt them to expand the headings by asking questions (e.g. *why is the brother given a game?*).

Blue Ask children what they think the problem is at the start of the story. How can they tell this problem has been solved at the end? Which chapter do they think contains the event that solved the problem?

2 yellow   Pupil's book page 57   copymaster 17

As for activity 1, using a more challenging contents list of chapters.

Guided group support Discuss the setting and characters – how might these change with each chapter? Focus on the detail that might go into each chapter..

Plenary Make a poster entitled 'What we know about chapters'. Ask children what they already know and what they have learnt today – for example:

- chapters divide long stories into shorter sections;
- you can take a break from reading at the end of each chapter;
- each chapter usually contains a major event;
- chapters can help authors to write stories in stages;
- some chapters have titles, but some have only numbers.

② Looking at issues in a story

Objectives   To explore the main issues in a story

To prepare children to write their own stories about issues

Shared session   *You need: OHT/poster 25.*

Take the opportunity to make any possible links with the RE or PSE programme children are currently following.

- Return to OHT/poster 25. Elicit the setting (Millie's house) and characters (Millie, Geraldine, Mum, Dad and Gran). Elicit the problem from the plan for the first chapter (Millie is jealous of her conceited cousin).

- Ask children what they think are the main issues in the story (e.g. children being mean to each other because of conceit on one side and jealousy on the other). Identify and underline parts of the plan which tell us this.

- Ask if this is a realistic story. Encourage children to see that it is by discussing real-life problems of jealousy or rivalry between siblings, cousins and friends.

- Explain that Michael Morpurgo's story may be about Millie and Geraldine, but that the main issues are deeper than this. These are real-life problems caused by conceit and jealousy.

- Brainstorm other real-life issues – for example, bullying, telling lies, stealing, family problems, racial or religious prejudice.

- Point out that authors often write stories about these issues (e.g. Jacqueline Wilson, Anne Fine). Have the children read any stories about the issues you have brainstormed?

Group follow-up activities

If you prefer, ask children to think of stories using other issues that are relevant to the class.

1 red   Pupil's book page 58   copymaster 18

Children look at pictures of two characters and a setting in the pupil's book. They read the story start about these characters on copymaster 18, and make notes about what happens next.

Guided group support Discuss the feelings of both characters, and how these might change in the story. Help children reflect this in their answers to the questions on copymaster 18.

2 blue/yellow   Pupil's book page 59

Children choose characters and a setting for a story from pictures in the pupil's book. They use the Hint! box to plan a story about a real-life issue.

Guided group support

Blue Ask children to think of further issues that might affect the characters in the pictures (think about the pictures of settings here, too). Decide on appropriate issues around which to plan a story.

Yellow As for the blue group. Discuss how the issue chosen affects the characters in different ways.

Alternative group activity   **red/blue/yellow**

Children look back at the contents pages for Session 1 (pupil's book pp. 56–57). They discuss what they think are the main issues in the story. They then think of a story about another real-life issue, and write a contents page for it.

Plenary   Discuss issues chosen in the follow-up activities. How would the children get these issues across in their stories? (e.g. choice of characters and setting; revealing characters' thoughts).

③ Planning the story

Objectives To revise the generic planning process already familiar to children

To extend this process to planning a story written in chapters

Shared session *You need: OHT/poster 26.*

■ Tell children they are going to write a class story, to be based on a real issue, and organised in chapters. They will also write their own stories in chapters. Establish whether children will write these on their own, in pairs or in small groups.

■ Identify the audience, and discuss how this will affect the stories (e.g. length, content, vocabulary). Identify how the finished stories will be published, and any opportunities for audience feedback.

■ Revise the link between planning a short story in paragraphs and planning a longer story in chapters. Establish why it is important to plan longer stories (e.g. there are more events, settings and characters so there is more chance of losing direction without planning).

■ Decide on the underlying issue for the story. Help children appreciate how an interesting story can be created around a serious issue. Here are some suggestions:

> 1 A new child comes to school. Some children are friendly towards him/her; others are hostile. The story investigates prejudice related to race, colour, creed, appearance or simply to 'outsiders'.

> 2 An empty plot of land on a housing estate is used by local children as a play area, but developers want to build a car park there. The children mount a campaign to turn the land into a park. The story investigates the different ways people want to use land.

■ When you have chosen an issue, use the left side of OHT/poster 26 to plan the story. Focus on the beginning, in chapter 1. Make brief notes about setting, characters and a problem. Decide on an event to introduce the main issue, and how to represent the inner thoughts and feelings of the characters in response. For suggestion 1 (above) this might be:

> **Setting**: a school (*give it a name and location*).

> **Character**: new pupil (*establish gender, age, general description*); other children.

> **Problem**: other children tease the new pupil.

> **Introducing the issue**: the initial setting takes place in class, as register is taken. Make it clear what it is about the new pupil that some other children object to.

■ Now consider the end of the story. Do children want the initial problem to be put right and the issue resolved? If so, discuss an appropriate resolution – for example:

> The other children realise the new pupil has a particular skill at something. One of the bullies asks the new pupil for help with this. The bully speaks out in defence of the new pupil. The other bullies see how horrible they have been.

- With a clear beginning and end, children will feel more confident about planning the events/chapters for the middle section. Plan between two and four. Emphasise the need for logical development and sequencing. For the story suggested above, your plan might look like this:

  Chapter 1 Monday morning, registration – introduction of issue.

  Chapter 2 Tuesday break-time – new pupil teased again.

  Chapter 3 Wednesday lunch-time – more teasing/other children are friendly.

  Chapter 4 Thursday afternoon – other children see new pupil's skill in class/games field.

  Chapter 5 Friday, after school – resolution.

Group follow-up activities

1 red   Pupil's book page 60   copymaster 19

Children use copymaster 19 to plan their own stories.

Guided group support Ensure children have a well-developed plan to support their future writing. Concentrate on four key related events that can be written up to slightly more length than usual for the group.

2 blue/yellow   Pupil's book page 60

Children use the framework in the pupil's book to plan their own stories.

Guided group support

Blue Focus on introducing the issue in the plan for the first chapter, through the problem or through description of characters. Discuss how the chapters can follow a sequence (e.g. the days of the week or a series of related events).
Yellow Encourage children to plan at least one additional chapter for their stories.

Plenary Discuss any successes and difficulties with the planning process. With the class, consider how particular problems can be solved.

④ Planning the detail in the story

Objectives To provide interesting details in each chapter to make the story entertaining and varied

To incorporate links between chapters to maintain continuity and encourage reader interest

Shared session *You need: OHT/poster 26 (from Session 3), large sheet of paper for class poster.*

 You may wish to conduct this over two sessions.

- Recap your story plan from Session 3. Discuss similarities to and differences from previous story plans children have made. Tell children you are going to think about additional details, to make the story interesting and entertaining, and not just a series of events.

- Ask children to think about books they have read as well as previous stories they have written. What details have made these stories interesting and readable? Make a class 'Story detail' poster to refer to in drafting sessions. Help children consider the following:
  - changes in setting – place, time of day, weather;
  - supporting characters for the main characters to meet and talk to;
  - conversations – with different characters speaking in different 'voices';
  - reflection – characters' inner thoughts can be brought out in the narration or through dialogue;
  - extra events and background information to support the theme of the story;
  - creation of emotions – anger, suspense, humour, etc.

- Go back over each chapter in the story plan, and decide how one or more of these details can be included in each one. Use the right-hand side of OHT/poster 26. In the story plan suggested in Session 3 for example, the chapters could 'follow' the new child around different parts of the school: classroom, playground, library, computer room, dining hall, etc.

- Plan how each chapter could be divided into a series of descriptions, events, dialogues and so on, each requiring a paragraph of its own.

- Next, explain that chapters should be <u>linked</u> in some way, to keep readers interested in the story. Draw a parallel with TV soaps – discuss how episodes are linked to each other (e.g. by picking up on events from previous episodes; by ending in a **cliffhanger** to be resolved in the next episode).

- Ask children to contribute ideas on linking chapters, gained from reading and writing experience. Write these up on the 'Story detail' poster, under the sub-heading 'How to link chapters'. Ideas may include:
  - a cliffhanger, which leaves us wondering what happens next;
  - finding a clue that has to be followed into the next chapter;
  - somebody asks a question that is answered in the next chapter;
  - a character changes location, and the story follows him/her into the next setting;
  - introducing a new character at the end of a chapter;
  - the link is triggered by an extra device – for example, a ringing telephone or a television report;
  - writing about the same event from another character's point of view.

- Plan some links between chapters in the class story. When finished, check over the whole plan to ensure these links make sense.

- Finally, decide on the narration and style of the story, reminding the class that this must suit the subject matter. For the narration, decide whether to use a first or third person viewpoint. Might there be separate narrators for each chapter? If so, how could each one be introduced?

- Decide whether or not you will write in the style of a story the class has read recently. Ask what might be an appropriate tone for the story: informal and chatty, or more serious? Note your decisions at the top of the plan.

Group follow-up activities

1 red   Pupil's book page 61

Children discuss links between episodes of a TV series or soap opera.

2 blue/yellow   Pupil's book page 61

Children look at the links between chapters 1–3 of a story plan for *Mystery in the boat-house*. They write in the links between chapters 3 and 4, then make up a plan for chapter 5, showing the links with chapter 4.

3 red   Pupil's book page 63   copymaster 19

Children use copymaster 19 from Session 3 to plan the details and links in their stories.

Guided group support Help establish supporting details to be included alongside each key event. Discuss how the stories might be developed. Ask children to draw annotated illustrations of the main characters, to support detailed descriptions in their writing.

3 blue/yellow   Pupil's book page 63

Children use their planning framework from Session 3 to plan the details and links in their stories.

Guided group support

Blue Help children develop the issue in the story through the way events are introduced and commented upon, and by revealing the inner thoughts and emotions of key characters. Help them create convincing links between chapters, and a convincing progression throughout the whole text.

Yellow As for the blue group. Work to establish an appropriate 'voice' for the text and consider the narrative viewpoint.

Plenary Recap why stories, and especially longer stories, benefit from additional details and links between chapters. Ask children for examples they have used.

5 Drafting the story

Objectives To sustain the writing of an extended text over a number of sessions

To write extended text from a detailed plan

Shared session *You need: OHT/poster 26, class posters from Sessions 1 and 4, large sheets of paper.*

*1 See **Drafting** on page 6 for more detailed advice on conducting a whole-class drafting session.*

2 An extended story in chapters cannot be accomplished in a single writing session. To reinforce understanding of what chapters are, and how they work, it is advisable to draft one chapter per session.

*3 To save time in the **Revising and editing** session, you may want to check the spelling and grammar in the class story as you work.*

- Recap the class story plan on OHT/poster 26. Revise the importance of keeping to a plan when writing a longer story. As the shared writing proceeds, keep children focused on the original plan, unless good alternative ideas are suggested. If this does occur, annotate and amend the original plan before proceeding with the writing.

- Recap the intended audience, and how this will affect the story. Recap the decisions made about narrative point of view, style and tone.

- For chapter beginnings, revise ways of creating interesting openings (see **How to write a historical story**, pp. 33–34). Brainstorm different ways to open a story (e.g. action, dialogue, description of character or setting). Decide on one for this chapter. Write the opening paragraph and follow the details in the plan.

- Focus on the variations between chapters in the plan (e.g. different events, settings, characters). Consider how these can be presented to the audience – is additional information needed for new settings or characters? Try to open and close chapters differently each time.

- At the beginning and end of each shared writing session, discuss how well you are making the vital links between chapters. These links are unlikely to 'just happen', and will probably involve some on-the-spot revisions.

■ After drafting each chapter, read it back to the class. This will help children to develop a 'feel' for what a chapter is. It will also be a good opportunity to consider chapter titles.

Group follow-up activities

Independent writing time is likely to be longer here than in previous units, allowing for more guided writing sessions. You may find your guided focus changes as children's writing progresses.

red/blue/yellow

Children work on the draft of their stories, using their plans.

Guided group support

Red Revise the point that a chapter is an extended 'chunk' of text, containing a number of paragraphs. Ask children to write a small number of paragraphs for each chapter. Help them extend chapter-length only when this will not cause loss of control.

Blue Prompt children to recall story language from known texts, and to use this in their writing. Focus on the details and language required to evoke the differences between settings, characters, etc. in different chapters.

Yellow Make sure children select vocabulary carefully. Encourage the use of thesauruses and word banks to investigate the best possible words. Focus on ways to develop the issue of the story (e.g. through events, dialogue, character's inner thoughts).

Plenary Discuss any problems or successes children have in expanding their plans into chapters. Compare and contrast planning and writing short stories with longer ones. Add points to the 'What we know about chapters' poster under the sub-heading 'What we have found out about writing chapters'.

6 Revising and editing the story

Objectives To enhance variety between chapters

To clarify links between chapters

To ensure cohesion in the story, and the way in which the issue is presented

Shared session *You need: story drafts, class poster from Session 4, large sheets of paper.*

*1 See **Revising and editing** on page 6 for more detailed advice.*
2 For time reasons, you may decide that this step is a lesser priority for this unit.

■ Choose one or more of the following as your revision focus:

- **The start of each chapter.** How well does it draw the reader into the story? Look at the opening lines and replace any over-used or inappropriate words with high-impact alternatives. Consider authorial questions, which highlight the issue in the story – for example:

  Would they give him a chance to fit into the new class? What would the so-called 'gang leaders' make of that weird haircut, and the way-out clothes?

- **The end of the story.** Discuss the resolution of the problem. Ask if the ending shows a suitable development of the issue from the beginning. You may decide to 'echo' the beginning in the ending – for example:

  Beginning
  The new kid got off to a really bad start in our class. He was led into the room by smarmy Liam, just as Mrs Robinson was shouting at everyone for not doing their homework.

> **Ending**
> So, in the end, the bad effects of the bad start wore off. Liam was still smarmy and Mrs Robinson still shouted at everyone for not doing their homework, but a few people learned a few things about how to treat new kids. Especially kids as unusual as Tom.

○ **The links between chapters.** Identify and underline words and phrases that link one chapter to the next, and to what has gone before. Ask whether they are effective. Change any words or phrases as necessary. Use the 'Story detail' poster from Session 4 to ensure that a variety of linking devices have been used.

Group follow-up activities

red/blue/yellow

Children revise their stories.

Guided group support Use the focus of the shared session here. Read through stories, considering if anything needs to be changed or added to get the issue across effectively.

Plenary

Ask volunteers to read out draft and revised versions of passages from their stories. Ask them why they chose to make particular changes. As a class, discuss the effectiveness of these changes. Ask children to suggest ways to improve weak links or uninteresting passages of description.

7 Publishing the story

Objectives

To bring work to the attention of the target audience

To investigate presentational methods

To illustrate and enhance text

Shared session

You need: final version of class story (see below), book-making materials (optional – see below).

*1 See **Publishing** on page 7 for more detailed notes on the issues involved in the final presentation of the text.*

2 To make the finished story like a 'real book', copy out the chapters, cover, contents page and illustrations on to loose sheets of paper. Slot them into a plastic book spine with protective acetate outer sheets. You may wish to link this with work in design and technology.

3 Write out the finished copy of the class story beforehand. Ask children to produce illustrations for the story in advance of this session (see the homework suggestion to follow Session 6).

■ Decide where the illustrations should go, and whether they will fit into spaces in the text, or need separate pages.

■ When you have finished laying out the text and illustrations, number all the pages. Now consider the contents page for the story.

■ Discuss the cover for the book. Decide on a title for the complete story. If possible, incorporate one of the children's illustrations.

■ Think about a blurb for the back cover. Ask what information usually goes in blurbs (e.g. story synopsis; possibly a description of the type of reader who will enjoy the story). Consider the intended audience and how you can establish the issue presented in this story. Write the blurb together.

■ Tell children to follow the layout of the class story in their own stories.

Group follow-up activities

You may wish to provide children with the following to help them write their finished versions:

- writing paper with erasable outer margins (you may wish to number these);
- line-guides to go underneath writing paper;
- a blank sheet to use as a contents page;
- an outer cover of folded cartridge paper;
- erasable writing pens to allow mistakes to be corrected.

red/blue/yellow

Children neatly write up and illustrate their stories. They then follow the stages in the shared session to 'publish' their work.

Guided group support

Red Encourage children to supplement their stories with illustrations. Help them to number the pages in their stories and write the contents page.

Blue Help children write short, interesting blurbs for the back cover, focusing on the key elements of the story, as well as the underlying issue. Point out the difference between a summary and a blurb: focus on the promotional elements of blurbs and the way they raise interest without supplying too many answers.

Yellow As with the blue group. Encourage children to include biographical details about the author for the inside front cover.

Plenary

Children present their finished books to the class, and/or prepare to present it to their intended audience. Once this audience has seen the books, their reactions can be discussed in class.

ADDITIONAL SESSIONS

Writing an alternative ending

Objectives

To investigate the impact of a story ending

To rewrite the ending of a text so that its impact is changed

To consider how the alternative ending changes the readers' view of characters and events

Shared session

You need: OHT/poster 25, a large sheet of paper marked up with a simple three-column grid (headings: Response to original ending/Alternative ending/How this changes views of characters and events) – see example below, a large clean sheet of paper.

- Use OHT/poster 25 to recap the story and issues in *Red Eyes at Night*.

- Ask children to think about the story from Millie's viewpoint. Does she have a good reason to be upset about Geraldine coming to stay every summer? Consider Geraldine's personality, and the way she takes over Millie's home.

- Discuss how well Mum and Gran handle the situation – are they being tactless? Are they asking too much of Millie, who is expected to take a lot of responsibility for looking after her cousin?

- Think about the story from Geraldine's viewpoint. Why does she have to spend every summer with Millie's family? Why can't she be with her own parents? Does she <u>have</u> any parents? Suggest that, possibly, Geraldine is secretly jealous of Millie.

■ Look at the plan for the final chapter. Discuss the reconciliation between the two girls. Do children feel this 'happy ending' is satisfying? Does Geraldine's ghost trick serve Millie right, or should Mum now tell Geraldine off as well? Ask if this makes Geraldine seem more or less likeable.

■ Now use your three-column grid. In the first column, make notes about how children feel about the ending of the story and why.

■ Ask children how they might change this ending to achieve an opposite effect. Write this in the second column of the grid.

■ Then ask if this alternative ending changes any views about the characters and events in the original story. Write this in the third column – for example:

Response to original ending	Alternative ending	How this changes views of characters and events
Millie deserves to have a trick played back on her by Geraldine.	Millie is so scared by Geraldine's ghost trick that she faints – injures head on floor.	Geraldine has problems at home and is jealous of Millie.
Geraldine's trick proves she is not so 'goody-goody' and has a sense of humour.	Mum and Gran very angry with Geraldine and tell her to go home.	Millie is generous, despite the tricks she plays on her cousin.
Possibly the two girls have more in common than they realise.	Millie finds out that Geraldine is unhappy at home, and asks Mum to let her stay.	Frightening people can be dangerous – someone can get hurt.

■ Write a version of the alternative ending with the whole class.

Group follow-up activities

1 red/blue   Pupil's book page 64

Children copy out and complete the chart in the pupil's book. They then write the last paragraph of their alternative ending for *Red Eyes at Night*.

Guided group support

Red Take a small focus and work on a directly 'opposite' ending (e.g. change Millie's reaction to the ghost trick, so that the girls become even more hostile to one another).

Blue Ask children to consider the story from either Millie's or Geraldine's viewpoint. Consider how this character wants the others to feel about them. Decide how the original ending will need to be changed in order to achieve this effect.

2 yellow   Pupil's book page 64

As for activity 1, but children think of two alternative endings. They then choose one and write the last paragraph of the alternative ending.

Guided group support Discuss how to make readers angry with either Geraldine or Millie at the end of the story. Encourage children to start by identifying the way they want the audience to feel, and then decide how to rewrite the story to achieve this.

Plenary Children read their alternative endings to the class. Ask those listening how these endings affect their views of characters and events in the original story. Ask the author of each ending if these views are the ones they expected.
(You may like to collate these alternative endings in a file, entitled 'Our Book of Endings'.)

Experimenting with poetry

Objectives   To look at different poetry styles and structures

To consider that some poetic forms create particular moods

Shared session   *You need: OHT/poster 27, 3 large sheets of paper for class poster.*

■ Tell children they are going to read three short poems. For each one, you want them to think about the shape of the poem, the subject matter and how it makes them feel.

■ Display OHT/poster 27 and read the first poem, masking the others. What do the children think it is about? Do they like it? Why? Why not?

■ Explain that this poem is called a **haiku** – a Japanese poetry form with a very precise structure. Identify this structure with the children:

  ◉ three short lines;

  ◉ seventeen syllables in total;

  ◉ five syllables in the first and third lines;

  ◉ seven syllables in the second line.

■ Ask children what else they notice about the shape and style of this poem (e.g. it does not rhyme, has no obvious beat or rhythm and contains no word-play).

■ Discuss how the style and structure of the poem add to its serious, thought-provoking tone. Do children think it was written for reading silently or for performing aloud? Consider what kind of audience it was written for (e.g. adults or older children, people interested in protecting the environment).

■ Warn children that the second poem is very different from the one you have just read. Read it, keeping the final poem masked. Discuss responses and some differences between this and the haiku.

■ Elicit the name of this sort of poem (**limerick**). Identify the structure with the children:

  ◉ five lines;

  ◉ the third and fourth lines are shorter than the others, so the rhythm changes;

  ◉ AABBA rhyme scheme;

  ◉ the first and last lines have the same rhythm and the same final word.

■ Discuss the nonsensical subject matter. Establish that limericks are meant to be entertaining and amusing. This is helped by the repetitive rhythm and clear rhymes.

■ Ask whether this limerick is for reading silently or for performing aloud. Point out that the repetitive rhythm is easy to sing or clap along to. Consider possible audiences and occasions for reciting this poem (e.g. to make someone laugh).

■ Now read the third poem. Discuss the subject matter. Ask children for differences and similarities with the other poems. Establish that this poem has:

  ◉ a simple verse structure and rhyme scheme (**rhyming couplets**);

  ◉ a strong beat;

  ◉ different rhythm in each verse.

■ Ask children why they think the rhythm changes in each verse (e.g. to recall the sounds made by a steam engine going up different gradients).

■ Discuss the intended audience for this poem. Discuss whether it should be read silently or spoken aloud. Consider whether the changing rhythm makes this poem difficult to perform aloud, and how a performer might manage the sound effects.

■ Ask children how this poem makes them feel. Establish that rhyming couplets can be used to create a variety of moods, while haiku and limericks tend to create a particular type of mood.

Group follow-up activities

1 red   Pupil's book page 65

Children copy two limericks into their books. They count the number of syllables in each line, and mark the rhyming words.

Guided group support Focus on the fixed form and style of limericks.

2 blue   Pupil's book page 66

Children read another poem describing the motion of a train, again in rhyming couplets. They consider similarities and differences between this poem and 'Night Mail'.

Guided group support Recap on points made about the structure, rhythm, content and tone of 'Night Mail'. Find the same elements in this poem.

3 yellow   Pupil's book page 67

Children look at three haiku. They check the number of syllables and think about the images used. They choose one of the haiku and write a second verse to go with it.

Guided group support   Recap on points made about the structure, content, tone and purpose of 'Haiku Moment'. Apply these points to the haiku in the pupil's book.

Plenary

Make a poster entitled 'Different forms of poetry'. Recap the points about haiku, limericks and rhyming couplets. This should include details of structure, rhythm and tone for each form. Ask children what else they have found out about these forms from their activity work.

Volunteers can perform the poems they have read. Those listening compare and contrast the performances, referring to the structure and content of the poems read, as well as their sound impact.

 Writing poetry

Objective   To write poems, experimenting with different styles and structures

Shared session   *You need: OHT/poster 27, class poster (from previous session), large sheets of paper for drafting.*

■ Tell children they are going to write poems for a class poetry collection. Establish the audience for this collection (e.g. another class, the whole school). Explain that children can choose to write poems in the style of a haiku, a limerick or in rhyming couplets.

■ Suggest that you work together on a poem in rhyming couplets – this will revise work on rhythm and rhyme.

- Recap that rhyming couplets can create a variety of moods, both serious and light-hearted. Recap the subject matter of 'Night Mail' (a description of a train journey). Suggest a transport theme for your poem, such as a car on a long holiday journey or a fire engine rushing to put out a fire.

- Establish that 'Night Mail' contains short couplets relating to different parts of the journey. Discuss different parts of the journey in your poem (e.g. racing along country roads or driving carefully through city streets). Plan four or five parts of the journey, one for each couplet.

- Brainstorm words and ideas, as well as rhyming pairs of lines. Any suggestions not used now will support children in their independent work.

- Consider how 'Night Mail' opens with a couplet that introduces the train and the purpose of its journey. Your opening couplet might look like this:

> Here is the car with the dusty chrome,
> Bringing the sun-tanned family home,

or

> Here is the fire engine, red and dashing,
> Racing to fight where the flames are flashing,

- Now move on to compose couplets which give the impression of moving at different speeds. Challenge children to use more or fewer syllables in these lines, to increase or decrease the speed. For example, the fast part of a car journey might be:

> Turning tyres burning, spinning spokes whirring,
> Whizzing past farms, outlines blurring,

The slow part of a fire engine's journey could be:

> On High Street – stop, go,
> Blue light off, wheels slow,

- Continue in this way until sufficient verses have been composed. As you work, read the poem back to the children, to maintain a sense of tone and style.

Group follow-up activities

Depending on the confidence of your class, give children a free choice of poetic form, or allocate particular forms to the various groups.

red/blue/yellow

Children write their own poems.

Guided group support Revise features of the chosen form, and help children stay on track as they write.

Alternative group activities

1 red/blue/yellow   Pupil's book page 68

Children choose the correct rhyming words to complete the couplets in 'White Fields'.

2 red/blue/yellow   Pupil's book page 69

Children rewrite a limerick, so that the lines rhyme and the rhythm is improved.

3 red/blue/yellow   Pupil's book page 69

Children write a haiku about an animal. They brainstorm a list of words and put them in columns depending on the number of syllables. They then write these words as short lines of five or seven syllables, to make a haiku.

Plenary Use this time for trouble-shooting any problems encountered by groups or individuals. Encourage children to work together to solve difficulties with rhyme scheme, rhythm, etc. Ask volunteers to read parts of their poems they feel have worked well.

Revising poems

Objective For children to write and revise poems for a particular purpose and audience

Shared session *You need: poem drafts, class poster from previous session (optional).*

- Tell children you are going to revise and edit poems to an excellent standard before presenting them.

- Revision focuses for the session include:
  - using different words or combinations of words to achieve the best effect;
  - adding, deleting and substituting words to make sure that the poem is as effective as possible;
  - improving rhyme and rhythm.

- As you revise, read the poem aloud to listen for changes made. Relate these changes to the desired tone for each couplet. Clap out the beat and rhythm. Identify the number of beats to a line, and the rhythm of the poem.

- Discuss whether you need to add or take out syllables to make the rhythm clearer, and to make a distinct difference between couplets. If necessary, use a thesaurus to find synonyms with more or fewer syllables that can be substituted to ensure the right rhythm.

Group follow-up activities **red/blue/yellow**

Children revise their poems.

Guided group support

Red Ensure children's poems 'fit' their chosen poetic form. Work on the number of syllables and/or rhythm and rhyme. Encourage use of a thesaurus to find high-impact vocabulary, as well as synonyms with the correct number of syllables.

Blue Encourage children to use adventurous/unusual vocabulary in their poems, that fits better with the chosen rhythm or rhyme scheme.

Yellow Consider how poems can be improved for the intended audience. Challenge children to maximise the intended tone of their poems.

Plenary Children read their drafted and revised poems to the class. Ask them to identify the changes made, and to give reasons for them. Ask those listening to comment constructively on the changes.

Homework suggestions

- Design your own planning grid for a story in chapters. Fill in the grid with details of any story you choose – it can be a well-known story or one you have made up yourself. **(After Session 1)**

- Ask an adult to read the local newspaper with you. Identify a list of issues that are affecting your community. **(After Session 2)**

- Identify an issue that is important to you or to people you know. Write a questionnaire to find out how people feel about this issue. Try this out on a few people, and make notes of their answers. Use your notes to help you plan a story about this issue. **(After Session 2)**

- Draw a picture to go with the class story. It should illustrate a setting, character or event in the story. **(After Session 6)**

- Look at a selection of story-books. Read the blurbs and find out whether any of them are about important issues. Make a list of any issues you find. **(After Session 7)**

- Rewrite the ending for a well-known story so that readers will feel very differently about the main character (e.g. Snow White does not marry the prince. She stays with the dwarves, but turns into a grumpy old woman and makes their lives a misery by nagging them!). **(After 'Writing an alternative ending')**

- Choose a story in chapters from your school or local library. Make sure the story examines a real-life issue. Keep a reading journal. At the end of each chapter summarise what it was about, who was in it and where it was set. Write down how the author examines the issue. Give your opinions about the book. Say what you think about the issue, and whether it affects you or not.

- Choose a favourite book that is written in chapters. Copy out the contents page and write a summary for each chapter beneath its heading or number. If the chapters do not already have titles, write some of your own.

UNIT **5** How to write a story in chapters

Colour the right number of stars to show how well you did the following things:

0 stars = I didn't do it.   3 stars = I did it well.
1 star = I gave it a try.   4 stars = I did an excellent job!
2 stars = I did it quite well.

I created detailed and interesting settings.	☆	☆	☆	☆
I included detailed character portraits.	☆	☆	☆	☆
I wrote a much longer story than usual.	☆	☆	☆	☆
I used chapters to organise the flow of the narrative.	☆	☆	☆	☆
Each of my chapters contained a clear section of the story.	☆	☆	☆	☆
I created 'hooks' and other links between chapters.	☆	☆	☆	☆
I varied the chapters by changing character or setting as well as events.	☆	☆	☆	☆
I gave my chapters numbers and/or titles to help readers find their way through the story.	☆	☆	☆	☆

Something I am especially pleased with

Something my audience liked in my writing

Something I'd like to do better next time

Term three non-fiction focus:
6 How to write a persuasive text

What most children will already know:

How to distinguish between fact and opinion

How to identify some different types of texts

How to scan texts to locate key words and phrases and how to use these to summarise text

How paragraphs are used to organise and sequence information

What children will learn in this unit:

How to identify persuasive writing

How to construct a piece of persuasive writing with an introduction, linked points, supporting evidence and a concluding summary

1 Identifying persuasive writing

Objectives
To investigate the three main structural elements of a piece of persuasive writing

To identify some of the vocabulary commonly found in persuasive writing

Shared session
You need: OHT/poster 28, 3 different colour OHT pens.

The content of the model text for this session links with QCA geography unit 8 'Improving the Environment'.

- Display the picture across the bottom of OHT/poster 28 (covering up the text) and ask children what issue they think the text is going to be about.

- Then reveal the first paragraph and read it together.

- Ask children to identify whether this is non-fiction or fiction. Can they tell you more specifically what type of text this is? To help them, ask what they think its **purpose** is (to **persuade** people that paper is wasted at school and also to take action to reduce the waste).

- Who do they think the writer might be, and who might they be trying to persuade?

- Explain that this introductory paragraph contains the writer's **opening statement** of their position (*We waste too much paper at school...We must try to reduce the amount of paper that we use*). Ask a volunteer to draw a coloured box around the first paragraph on the OHT and label it 'Introduction (opening statement)'.

- Do the children agree with the writer? Explain that the writer will go on to develop an **argument** (linked **points** with supporting **evidence** – reasons, facts, examples). What points do they think the writer might put forward?

- Now reveal and read together the second paragraph. Do any of the points match the children's own ideas? Ask a volunteer to box and label (in a different colour) this paragraph 'Argument (points + evidence)'.

- Look at the final paragraph, which reinforces the author's opening position (stressing again the main point of the argument) in the form of a **closing statement**. Ask a volunteer to box and label this paragraph 'Conclusion (closing statement)'.

■ Now focus on some examples of the language typically used in persuasive writing, in particular:

- **logical connectives** which help to link ideas/show cause and effect (e.g. *so, because, however, therefore* and the construction *If...then...*);

- phrases such as *we need to, we must, we should* which the writer uses to state their opinion of what should be done.

■ Ask children to identify and underline examples of all of these in the model text. Point out, also, the use of the **present tense.**

Group follow-up activities

1 red/blue   Pupil's book page 70   copymaster 20

Using copymaster 20, children separate a piece of persuasive writing into its three sections, pick out the two main points of the argument and finally identify examples of typical persuasive vocabulary.

Guided group support Make sure children understand the three sections that they are looking for and, in particular, can distinguish the two main points from the supporting evidence. Encourage them to write what each section should contain (e.g. introduction: opening statement of point of view).

2 blue/yellow   Pupil's book page 71

Children read a piece of persuasive writing and decide together which section is the introduction, the argument and the conclusion. In their books, they write down the two main points of the argument along with the supporting evidence for each point. Finally, they identify examples of persuasive vocabulary in the text.

Guided group support Ask children to suggest some alternative or additional connectives that could be used in this piece of writing.

Plenary

Make a poster entitled 'Persuasive writing'. Tell children that over the next few lessons they are going to write down what they have learnt about this type of writing. Ask them to help you note down the three main sections of the text you have read. Use the same colours that you used to mark the paragraphs
Then write 'Special vocabulary' and ask children to help you write up the words and phrases you have identified. Brainstorm as many logical connectives as you can think of, including sentence openings such as *However..., Therefore..., Finally...* Add any new vocabulary to the checklist.
Can children suggest anything else to add (e.g. use the present tense)?

② Ordering and linking points in an argument

Objectives

To use language appropriate to an argument

To use evidence and examples to support a point of view

To link points in an argument so that one follows on from another

Shared session

You need: OHT/poster 29 , 3 different colour OHT pens, a large sheet of paper.

■ To introduce the session, ask children whether they think it is a good idea to give someone a pet as a present. Then explain that you are going to show them a statement from an animal welfare centre about the problems that can arise. Ask children to think of some points which the statement might include and spend a few minutes noting down their ideas.

- Display OHT/poster 29. Can children identify the main points and the supporting evidence given? Underline the points and evidence in two different colours to distinguish them.

- Next, ask children to look for and underline any vocabulary that is commonly used in persuasive writing.

- Can children now add some more points to this argument (with supporting evidence)? Refer back to their earlier ideas. Encourage them to think of 'evidence' sentences (i.e. points that can be backed up with a *because* statement – *It is cruel to keep a large dog in a small flat **because** they need space to run around*).

- Ask children to choose the most important points to add to the existing text (limit this to about three). Discuss where these points would fit best in the text. Begin to produce a class text on a large sheet of paper or blank OHT.

- Now develop these points more fully with appropriate logical connectives and phrases such as *we should, we must, the reason why...*

- To give children more practice in creating 'evidence' sentences, play a game where one child makes a statement and another has to develop it with an example or justification – for example, *Children should walk to school because...; You should eat more fruit because...* You could make this more fun by starting with a 'silly' statement that has to be justified – for example, *Children should be paid to come to school because...; Football should not be shown on TV because...*'

Group follow-up activities

1 red   Pupil's book page 72

Children complete some 'evidence' sentences, using given connectives.

2 red   Pupil's book page 72

Children work in pairs to come up with points to make an argument.

Guided group support Encourage children to provide evidence to support their points.

3 blue   Pupil's book page 72

Children sort lines of an argument into an ordered sequence.

Guided group support Remind children to read all the sentences before beginning to sequence them.

4 blue   Pupil's book page 73

As for activity 2, but children are also asked to put their points in order of importance and to use appropriate connectives.

Guided group support Remind children to make their points in order of importance.

5 yellow   Pupil's book page 73

Children reorder the main part of an argument adding in appropriate connectives.

6 yellow   Pupil's book page 73

Children work in pairs to write an argument, providing supporting evidence and using appropriate connectives.

Plenary Children share their arguments with the class. Ask those listening to say which points they find most persuasive.

3 Introducing and concluding the persuasive writing

Objectives   To construct an introduction and a conclusion to a piece of persuasive writing

To summarise the main point of the argument

Shared session   *You need: class text (from Session 2), writing board or flipchart, class poster (from Session 1).*

- Display the writing you produced in the last session and encourage children to tell you what is missing to make it a complete piece of persuasive writing (an introduction and conclusion).

- Invite children to help you write the introduction. Remind them that it should include an **opening statement**. It needs to be kept short and it must capture the reader's interest.

- To help children achieve this, ask them what they think is the main point to be argued. There is no single 'right' answer (e.g. *People should not give pets as presents*, or *It can be cruel to give a pet as a present*). Encourage children to think of a dramatic first sentence (e.g. *A pet is not a toy that can be thrown away if it is unwanted*).

- Write up suggestions on the board or flipchart. Ask children to help you choose the best one and challenge them to give you reasons for their choice.

- Explain that you are now going to write the conclusion. Ask children if they can remember what it should include (a **closing statement** of the main point of the argument which reinforces the opening statement).

- Remind children that the conclusion should be quite brief and to the point: it ties together the threads of the argument and finishes it off neatly.

- Suggest some appropriate ways to begin – for example, ***We have now shown you some of the reasons why it can be cruel to give a pet as a present*** or ***We have explained/ described...*** Again, encourage experiment and alternative ideas. Write up the ideas, encouraging and praising the use of suitable language and vocabulary.

- With the children, choose an ending for your piece of persuasive writing. Again, challenge them to explain why they think this is the best one.

Group follow-up activities   **1 red   Pupil's book page 74**

Children choose the best opening statement for two short arguments. They then think of points to add to the arguments, or to argue the opposite point of view.

Guided group support Encourage children to consider all the answers before making a choice. Some sentences are almost right. Discuss why one is better than another.

2 blue   Pupil's book page 75

Children write an opening statement for an argument. They then think of points to add to the argument.

Guided group support Encourage discussion about possible opening statements – for example, *Our school should have a swimming pool; It would be better for the children if the school had a swimming pool.*

3 yellow   Pupil's book page 76

Children write an introduction and a conclusion to an argument. They then think of points to add to the argument, or to argue the opposite point of view.

Guided group support Remind children to keep the opening and closing statements short. Encourage discussion about possible closing statements before completing the written work.

Plenary   Add information about introductions and conclusions to the class poster – for example:

- **Introduction**: opening statement of position, must be brief, capture reader's attention.
- **Conclusion**: final statement of main point of argument, keep it brief, finish with something memorable.

Ask children for their ideas, too.

4 Planning the persuasive text

Objective   To plan a piece of persuasive writing

Shared session   *You need: writing board or flipchart, class poster (from Session 1).*

For this session it would be helpful to have a copy of your school's official prospectus for parents. The children are going to create a prospectus of their own but aimed at other children rather than at parents. If you prefer, you could adapt the ideas for this session to create another sort of brochure – for example, for a local place of interest.

- Show children the school prospectus. Look at the ways in which it tries to persuade parents to send their children to the school – for example, it might mention academic achievements, facilities, or after-school activities.

- Ask children to help you write a list of their favourite things about their school – perhaps the playground or playing field, school clubs and societies, lessons or equipment they particularly like – even school dinners!

- Now develop some of the points more fully with logical connectives. Make sure that each sentence includes a feature of the school and a benefit of that feature (e.g. *You will like our school **because** it has a big playground **so** you can play exciting games with all your friends at playtime*).

- Encourage children to help you think of an introduction to the prospectus (e.g. *It is great at St Catherine's School –you will have fun and make lots of friends*). Think about how to sum up and conclude the prospectus (e.g. *Now you can see it is the best school around, ask your parents to send you here straight away!*).

Group follow-up activities   Children plan their own school prospectus. They make lists of all of the most appealing features of the school and plan how to set these out in a booklet or zigzag book.

Guided group support

Red Work with children to help them think of attractive features of the school that would help persuade other children to choose it.

Blue/Yellow Remind children to develop the points made with examples or evidence.

Plenary   Ask children to read out their ideas. Comment on and praise the use of logical connectives to expand and develop 'evidence'.

5 Drafting the persuasive text

Objectives To draft the writing from a plan

To use a thesaurus to improve vocabulary, strengthening the argument

Shared session *You need: class plan (from Session 4), a large sheet of paper.*

*See **Drafting** on page 6 for more detailed advice on conducting a whole-class drafting session.*

■ Begin by referring to the notes which you made for the school prospectus in the last session. Read them through with the children.

■ Ask children to suggest how the writing needs to be developed. Encourage them to be systematic – begin by adding to the introduction and go on to develop the listed points more fully.

■ Encourage children to try to improve the original vocabulary. Suggest looking in a thesaurus for ideas – for example, *great* could be changed to *wonderful/magnificent/superb*.

■ Develop the closing statement into a paragraph. Include sufficient detail but do not make it too long.

■ Re-read the text with children. Emphasise that it has now been drafted but is not yet finished.

Group follow-up activities Children work on drafting their own writing using a thesaurus.

Guided group support

Red Use one child's plan and draft a piece of group writing. Act as scribe for the group.

Blue Help children to develop their introductions and conclusions so that they link well with the main points raised in the text.

Yellow Encourage children to use the thesaurus once they have drafted their work, to improve or extend vocabulary.

Plenary Ask children to suggest alternatives to over-used words (e.g. *nice, good, said*) and look them up in a thesaurus.
Comment on and praise the use of interesting and imaginative vocabulary in the children's own writing.

6 Revising and editing the persuasive text

Objective To edit the persuasive writing

Shared session *You need: class draft (from Session 5), different colour marker pens.*

*See **Revising and editing** on page 6 for more detailed advice.*

■ Check spellings and punctuation.

■ Look carefully at layout and presentation. Use examples of children's work to point out good use of spacing, paragraphing and other presentational devices.

■ Consider the use of bullet points for the main part of the argument, to separate different ideas.

- Check that the points made are linked by suitable connectives.
- Look again at the vocabulary and encourage children to make suggestions for possible improvements.

Group follow-up activities   Children revise and edit their own prospectuses.

Guided group support

Red   Remind children to use a dictionary to check spellings. Encourage them to think about layout and presentation, particularly paragraphing.

Blue   Encourage children to look carefully at their use of persuasive vocabulary and of connectives to link points.

Yellow   Ask children to look carefully at their use of vocabulary and discuss possible improvements. Remind children to think about presentation – for example, bullet points, use of headings.

Plenary   Ask volunteers to describe one of the changes they have made to their own work.

---

7 Publishing the persuasive text

Objective   To publish the persuasive writing

Shared session   *You need: class text, folded sheets of A4 paper, computer and word-processing software (optional).*

*See **Publishing** on page 7 for more detailed notes on the issues involved in the final presentation of the text.*

- Use the text developed in previous shared sessions, and encourage children to think carefully about layout and presentation.
- First, look at the layout of the original school prospectus. It may have illustrations or photographs interspersed with text. The text may have bullet points or headings and sub-headings.
- Discuss how children could plan the layout of their own prospectus. (The simplest forms are 'zigzag' books or folded sheets of A4.)
- You could begin by thinking about the design of the front cover.
- Discuss the use of illustrations.
- If the children are to publish their work using a word-processing package, encourage them to consider an appropriate font and font size.

Group follow-up activities   Children work on publishing their own writing.

Guided group support

Red   Help children to plan the layout of their text. Encourage them to think of appropriate illustrations.

Blue   Remind children to think about how to organise the text with headings and sub-headings and to consider what these headings should look like. Encourage them to use captioned illustrations.

Yellow   Encourage children to think about the design, particularly how to emphasise different points in the text (e.g. using bold, italics, underlining, capitals, size of heading).

Plenary   Show examples of published work and ask for (positive) comments from the rest of the class.

ADDITIONAL SESSIONS

Matching the writing to the audience

Objective
To understand that a persuasive text can be presented in different ways, depending upon its intended audience

Shared session
You need: OHT/poster 30, a large sheet of paper.

 In this session, children are asked to consider how a persuasive text may be presented in different ways. They go on to produce an 'advert' for a school fête. It may be appropriate to adapt the content of the lesson to suit a forthcoming school event. This would help to make the writing experience real and relevant for the children.

■ Read OHT/poster 30 with the children.

■ Analyse the different parts of the letter – the opening statement, argument and conclusion. Look for examples of persuasive language.

■ Now tell children that the headteacher has considered the argument and challenges them to raise the money for the playground equipment.

■ Think of some ways to raise money – for example, letters to businesses in the local community or an event held at school.

■ With children, plan a poster advertising a school fête to be held to raise money for the project. Include some of the 'evidence' from the letter but discuss how it needs to be altered so that the poster suits its purpose and audience – for example, *Climbing frames and balancing beams would also be good for our health because we would be exercising and getting fit* would be more appropriate on a poster as *Help your child get fit! Our playground needs improving* might change to *Save our playground!*

■ Discuss other information that needs to be included on the poster – a description of the event with information about time and place, etc.

Group follow-up activities
Children design their own posters to advertise the money-raising event – either the fête already discussed, or a real school event.

Guided group support Remind children to include examples of persuasive writing in their posters. These could be based either on the 'evidence' in the model text or on their own ideas.

Plenary
Comment on the posters the children have been working on. Look for and praise examples of effective persuasive writing.

Writing an advert

Objective
To apply the techniques of persuasive writing to writing an advert

Shared session
You need: OHT/poster 31.

■ Display OHT/poster 31 (a diagram of a fantasy house-cleaning machine) and explain that your task is to write a piece of persuasive text to make people buy the machine.

- Look at the name of the machine (and check that children understand what both words mean in this context). Explain the importance of eye-catching names in advertisements. Why do children think alliterative names work well? (They are memorable.)

- Ask children to think up a catchy slogan or heading for the advert – what do they think is the machine's key selling point? (e.g. *This machine will change your life forever! Now you can solve all your domestic problems!*).

- List the points that will form the development of your argument (e.g. *never have to dust, wash up, tidy, cook again; impress your friends with super-clean house; have extra time for fun*).

- Write a sentence for the closing statement (e.g. *You need the Demon Domestic in your life; Things will never be the same again if you buy a Demon Domestic*).

- Discuss how adverts are illustrated. The labelled diagram could be positioned at the top or in the middle of the writing. Small 'exploded detail' illustrations could be inserted effectively at other points in the text.

Group follow-up activities red/blue/yellow Pupil's book page 77

Children write their own advert based on a machine they have invented.

Guided group support

Red Help children think of a suitable fantasy machine so that they can concentrate on the writing.

Blue Encourage children to make brief planning notes for their writing

Yellow Allow children access to the checklist made in the shared session. Encourage brief planning notes.

Plenary Spend a few minutes listening to the children's ideas for fantasy machines. Challenge children to tell you five things that are needed in a persuasive text (e.g. opening statement, argument, supporting evidence, closing statement, special vocabulary).

Writing advertising slogans and jingles

Objective To summarise an argument and present it as a slogan or jingle

Shared session *You need: OHT/poster 32, a large sheet of paper.*

- Talk to children about radio adverts and jingles they have heard. Ask them to tell you some that they know. Ask why they think jingles are effective in advertising (e.g. they catch attention, sum up information and are easily remembered).

- Display and read OHT/poster 32.

- Talk about the 'evidence' in Willy Wonka's argument (e.g. no more shopping, no washing-up).

- Ask children to help you think up some advertising jingles to sell the chewing gum – for example:

> One chew and you'll be cheering!
> The gum that makes you say yum!
> Chew me for breakfast, dinner and tea!

■ Talk about the kinds of language commonly used in advertising – **rhymes**, **alliteration** and **puns** are all frequently used.

Group follow-up activities   **red/blue/yellow**   **Pupil's book page 78**

Children invent some advertising jingles and slogans for more of Willy Wonka's amazing sweets.

Guided group support   Encourage children to use rhyming dictionaries and thesauruses to improve their writing.

 Homework suggestions

- Collect examples of leaflets written to persuade. **(After Session 1)**
- Write a piece of text persuading teachers not to give out homework. **(After Session 3)**
- Write a leaflet to promote a local sports club or society like Brownies or Cubs. **(After Session 3)**
- Think up as many reasons as possible why the school should be closed on hot days. **(After Session 3)**
- Write two alternative arguments on the same theme – for example, for/against cycling to school, hot school dinners, watching TV. **(After Session 3)**

- Make a poster to advertise a forthcoming school event. **(After 'Matching the writing to the audience)**
- Look for puns and word-play in advertising slogans. Collect examples. **(After 'Writing advertising slogans, puns and jingles)**
- Listen to jingles on the radio. Tape record them or write them down. **(After 'Writing advertising slogans, puns and jingles)**

UNIT 6 How to write a persuasive text

Colour the right number of stars to show how well you did the following things:

0 stars = I didn't do it.   3 stars = I did it well.
1 star = I gave it a try.   4 stars = I did an excellent job!
2 stars = I did it quite well.

I identified the three main sections of a piece of persuasive writing.	☆	☆	☆	☆
I found out about the connecting words used in persuasive writing.	☆	☆	☆	☆
I wrote my own opening and closing statements.	☆	☆	☆	☆
I used the right kind of language in my argument.	☆	☆	☆	☆
I used evidence and examples to support my point of view.	☆	☆	☆	☆
I remembered to link my points together.	☆	☆	☆	☆
I tried to match my writing to my audience.	☆	☆	☆	☆
I summarised an argument.	☆	☆	☆	☆

Something I am especially pleased with

Something my audience liked in my writing

Something I'd like to do better next time

Name ....   Date ....

	Time
Beginning Characters: Setting: Problem:	
Middle Conflict/climax:	**Time**
End Resolution:	**Time**

Name ....

Date ....

Day

Week

Month

Seasons

Years

Name .... Date ....

Name _____

Age _____

Address _____

_____

Family _____

Draw a picture of your character here

Colour of hair _____   Colour of eyes _____

He/she is wearing _____

_____

_____

He /she likes to: fish   sew   weave   cook   make spears

play in the woods   play with friends   play by him/herself

look after the animals   chop wood

Any other interests _____

_____

_____

He/she is _____ because _____

_____

He/she is _____ because _____

_____

He/she is _____ because _____

_____

Name ....   Date ....

Read this story opening. It should be set in Anglo-Saxon times but the author has got muddled up. Some of the words belong in modern times.

"See you later," called Carly as she and her younger brother Tony leapt into the car.

"Take care now, and mind you get at least fifty pence for those apples at market," called their mother. The children waved goodbye, and fastened their track-suit tops tightly around them.

An hour later, the car sped into Melksham. Carly and Tony jumped out with their two plastic carrier bags and settled themselves in the market-place.

"Buy your apples, only fifty pence for four!" shouted Tony, trying to be heard above the noise of the cars, buses and lorries.

After a lunch of burger and chips, the children had only a few apples left to sell, and they were looking forward to going home. Suddenly there was an almighty noise and soldiers in tanks charged through the market-place, flashing their guns and screaming loudly.

Pick out the words which set this story in modern times. Change them for words which set it in Anglo-Saxon times.

Modern-day words	Anglo-Saxon words
Carly Tony	Ethelberga

Name ....

Date ....

Title:

Cast:

Scene 1

Setting:

Action:

Characters:

Scene 2

Setting:

Action:

Characters:

Scene 3

Setting:

Action:

Characters:

Scene 4

Setting:

Action:

Characters:

Name .... Date ....

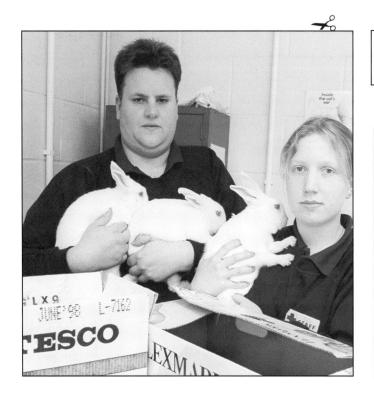

Abandoned... Welfare assistants Andrew Stripe and Sophie Bacctus with the rabbits dumped at the sanctuary

Three white bunnies did not have much to celebrate this Easter when they were dumped outside an animal shelter.

Easter misery as rabbits are dumped

They were found outside Cambridge's Blue Cross shelter in Garlic Row, on Bank Holiday Monday.

Centre Manager Alan Maskell said, "The three young rabbits were left at the gates in cardboard boxes and, despite the centre being open, staff were not informed they were there. Luckily, they were discovered before any harm came to them and safely taken in."

Mr Maskell said, "When they are ready for adoption, we will find the right homes for them where they can receive the love, care and attention they deserve."

Name .... Date ....

Headline

Orientation

Picture

Caption

Main body

Reorientation

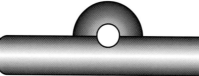

Name ....

Date ....

Title _____

Opening section: what the report is about

Information section

Heading 1 _____

Heading 2 _____

Heading 3 _____

Closing section: something interesting about the subject

Name ....   Date ....

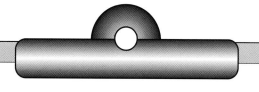

Main heading _____

First subheading

Second subheading

Name

Date

Title:

Verse 1: The journey there…

Verse 2: What the king sees…

Verse 3: What the king does…

Verse 4: The journey back…

Name .... Date ....

Write these chapter headings under the correct chapter. (The first three have been done for you.)

> *Back to normal*
> *A celebration*
> *The battle*
> *Facing danger*

Write what you think happens in each chapter.

Chapter	What happens
Chapter 1 *Once upon a time...*	It is brillig time in the forest. All the creatures are playing: the slithy toves, the borogoves and the mome raths.
Chapter 2 *The problem of the Jabberwock*	The wise old father talks to his son. He warns him of the dangerous creatures in the forest, especially the Jabberwock.
Chapter 3 *Looking for the monster*	
Chapter 4	
Chapter 5	
Chapter 6	
Chapter 7	

Name

Date

Draw boxes around the **opening section**, the **explanation of the process** and the **closing section**. Write the name of each section next to the box.

- - - - - - - - - - - - - - - - - - - -

New glass bottles are made mainly of silica sand. The sand is melted in a furnace, at a very high temperature. Recycled glass bottles are made in a similar way, but cost less and use up fewer natural resources.

- - - - - - - - - - - - - - - - - - - -

The process begins when people take their used bottles and jars to a bottle bank. Next, the bottles and jars are taken by lorry to a recycling plant. At the plant, bottle tops and lids are removed. After that, the glass is crushed into small pieces.

- - - - - - - - - - - - - - - - - - - -

The crushed glass is then sent by lorry to a bottle factory. Here, it is mixed with a small amount of silica sand. It is then melted in a furnace, at a lower temperature than new glass. Finally, the hot liquid glass is drawn out of the furnace and fed into machinery that makes it into bottles.

- - - - - - - - - - - - - - - - - - - -

Recycled glass is as pure and strong as new glass. Glass can be recycled many times without losing its quality.

When you have finished, write these **sub-headings** on the dotted line above the correct paragraph.

From the bottle bank to the recycling plant
The strength of recycled glass
The lower cost of recycling
Turning crushed glass into bottles

Name .... Date ....

Draw boxes around the **opening section,** the **explanation of the process** and the **closing section.** Write the name of each section next to the box.

- -

To grow beautiful flowers or tasty vegetables, gardeners often put compost in their soil. Compost is produced by allowing vegetable matter to decompose naturally.

- -

First the compost ingredients have to be collected. Any raw vegetable or plant material is suitable, including leaves, grass and vegetable peelings. To introduce helpful bacteria into the compost, some garden soil is also mixed in.

- -

Next, the compost mixture is put in a special composting bin, or piled up in the garden. The compost is then left alone for many months while nature does its work.

- -

Microbes, such as bacteria and fungi, soon begin to rot the vegetable material. As a side-effect, natural warmth is produced in the compost. This, in turn, helps to speed up the process. Eventually, natural decomposition transforms the waste vegetable material into soft brown compost.

- -

Gardeners either dig the compost into the soil or spread it on the surface. Compost replaces nutrients in the soil, because it contains nitrogen and other important elements.

When you have finished, write these **sub-headings** on the dotted line above the correct paragraph.

Collecting the ingredients for compost   The purpose of compost
How microbes rot the vegetable matter   Where to leave the compost mixture
How to use compost

Name .... Date ....

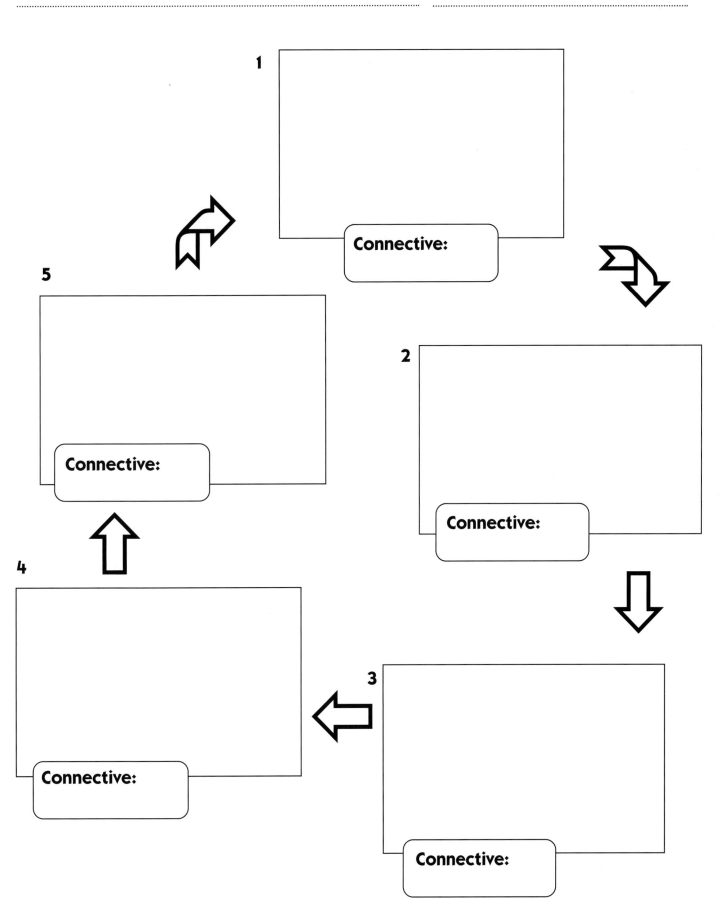

1

Connective:

5

Connective:

2

Connective:

4

Connective:

3

Connective:

Name .... Date ....

Material	How it is recycled	Advantages of recycling	How to encourage recycling
Plastic bottles			
Paper			
Drinks cans			
Glass bottles			
Vegetable waste			
Clothes			

Name .... Date ....

Write the chapter titles next to the beginning, middle or end sections.
Write notes about what you think happens in each chapter.

Story structure	Chapter title	What I think happens
Beginning		Characters: Setting: Problem:
Middle		Event: Event: Event: Climax:
End		Resolution:

Now think of a title for the story.

Name   Date

Read the beginning of this story.

It was a sunny day. Kids were playing football, skateboarding and just hanging around. No one noticed when Anna reached inside Danny's bag and pulled out his Walkman.

Make notes for the rest of this story.

1   How does Danny find out that Anna stole his Walkman?

2   How does Danny get his own back?

3   What happens next?

4   What happens in the end?

Name .... Date ....

Chapter 1 – beginning

Characters:

Setting:

Problem:

Issue:

Link:

Chapter 2 – events

What happens:

Link:

Chapter 3 – events

What happens:

Link:

Chapter 4 – events

What happens:

Climax:

Link:

Chapter 5 – ending

Resolution:

Link:

Name ....

Date ....

You should not eat too many sugary foods. Eating too much sugar is bad for your teeth and bad for your body.

Sugar is bad for your teeth because it causes tooth decay. Sugar makes a sticky substance called plaque grow. Plaque attacks your teeth and causes cavities. Your body does not need lots of sugar, so eating too much of it is also bad for your health. Therefore, try to eat lots of healthy foods instead that will give your body all the nutrients it needs.

As you have seen, too much sugar is bad for your health. So, try not to eat too many sugary foods!

Point 1

Point 2

PUBLISHED BY THE PRESS SYNDICATE OF THE UNIVERSITY OF CAMBRIDGE
The Pitt Building, Trumpington Street, Cambridge, United Kingdom

CAMBRIDGE UNIVERSITY PRESS
The Edinburgh Building, Cambridge CB2 2RU, UK
40 West 20th Street, New York, NY 10011-4211, USA
10 Stamford Road, Oakleigh, VIC 3166, Australia
Ruiz de Alarcón 13, 28014 Madrid, Spain
Dock House, The Waterfront, Cape Town 8001, South Africa

http://www.cambridge.org

First published 2001
Reprinted 2001

Printed in the United Kingdom by GreenShires Group Ltd, Kettering, Northamptonshire.

Typefaces Concorde, Frutiger, ITC Kabel   *System* QuarkXPress®

A catalogue record for this book is available from the British Library

ISBN 0 521 80547 3

Cover design by Traffika Publishing Ltd
Design by Peter Simmonett and Angela Ashton
Illustrations by Barry Ablett, Beccy Blake, Louise Alexandra Ellis, Amanda Hall, Sally Kindberg, Stephen Lambert, Sami Sweeten and Thomas Taylor

We would like to thank the following teachers and headteachers for their help on Cornerstones for Writing: Anne Allen, Lorna Ferry, Bonnie Kennedy, Jackie Lucas, Carol Meek and Susan Seed.

NOTICE TO TEACHERS
The copymasters and self-assessment sheets in this publication may be photocopied free of charge for classroom use within the school or institution which purchases the publication. Copymasters, self-assessment sheets and photocopies of them remain in the copyright of Cambridge University Press and such photocopies may not be distributed or used in any way outside the purchasing institution. Written permission is necessary if you wish to store the material electronically.

'Easter misery as rabbits are dumped' (photo and story on copymaster 6) reproduced by kind permission of the Cambridge Evening News.